# WIL

## *and*

# CELTIC PATHS

Tom Davies, a Welshman born and bred, trained as a journalist with the *Western Mail* and later worked for *The Sunday Times*, the *Sunday Telegraph* and *The Observer*, where for three years he was the diarist Pendennis. Now a writer, broadcaster and columnist on the *Western Mail*, he has written thirteen books: his *Merlyn the Magician and the Pacific Coast Highway* was short-listed for the Thomas Cook Travel Book of the Year Award, while his pilgrimage narrative *Stained Glass Hours*, here published in paperback for the first time as *Wild Skies and Celtic Paths*, won the Winifred Mary Stanford prize for the best book with a religious theme.

His other best-selling books for Triangle include *Landscapes of Glory* (1996) and *The Celtic Heart* (1997). *The Road to the Stars*, his account of a summer pilgrimage to Santiago de Compostela, will appear early in 1999.

He lives in a coastguard tower overlooking the Bristol Channel in Penarth, South Wales and is married with three sons.

*In memory
of
Canon David Watson
1933–1984
RIP*

# WILD SKIES
## *and*
# CELTIC PATHS

## TOM DAVIES

TRIANGLE

This edition first published in Great Britain in 1998
Triangle Books
Holy Trinity Church
Marylebone Road
London NW1 4DU

First published by New English Library in 1985

Copyright © Tom Davies 1998

British Library Cataloguing-in-Publication Data

A catalogue record for this book is available
from the British Library

ISBN 0-281-05190-9

Typeset by Pioneer Associates, Perthshire
Printed in Great Britain by
Caledonian International, Glasgow

# Contents

# 1

# The Kingdom of the Queen of Ice

——◆——

ELY · DOWNHAM MARKET · KING'S LYNN · WALSINGHAM

A strong north wind was blowing down over the Fens as I cycled along the road to Ely following a trail of half-eaten carrots. They kept on cropping up again and again on my Easter pilgrimage – long lines of carrots dotted every ten feet or so along the edge of the road. Occasionally a mouse, pancaked flat by a speeding car, broke up the orange line. Sometimes it was a mangled bird. Just by Deeping Fen a huge rat lay dead by the grass verge, its fat fleshy tail curled out behind it, a perfect smile of release twisted on its tiny white lips. Yet, quite soon, there were those carrots again.

All around me, in a vast sunken arena, lay the flatlands of the Fens; the finest agricultural soil in England, as you might have guessed from its deep black richness. The land lies so low you sometimes get the feeling that you are floating along in the air as you look out over the deep streams bisecting the black parallelograms of soil yet to yield the first signs of their crops.

This feeling of abstraction was reinforced by the sky; not so much one sky as three skies packed into one. All day those skies swirled around me as I pedalled into the teeth of the north wind. Here was a deep grey sky, full of weeping and endless lament. Over there was a thick black sky, full of biliousness as it prepared to fling yet another shower of cold Fen rain into my face. Somewhere between the two was yet another sky which was neither sun nor rain, neither fish nor fowl – a nothing sky unable to decide what shape it was going to be.

The odd hunched tree broke up the flatness of the land; sometimes a line of poplars marched across the horizon, much as they do in the wine-growing regions of France. It began raining again and a lorry roared past me, buffeting my side with the damp smack of its draught, the spray dancing around inside its four wheels like a trapped and angry ghost.

And there it was again – the gaunt Gothic outline of Ely Cathedral, spearing the packed Fen skies before disappearing into the rain mists again, haunting and elusive like a strange symbol in a recurring dream, huge and enigmatic, one great cannon for God.

All cathedrals have their own personalities. Some come on as sweet as a burst of applause, others have the aristocratic charms of an old and lovely lady. All too many are simply citadels of snootiness, a few even aspire to a teenage spriteliness. That rainy morning, though, each time I glimpsed her over the black fields and between the trees, Ely Cathedral kept changing her form. The nearer I got the more impressive she became, a massive Gothic birthday cake suspended from the rain clouds, a great Spanish galleon riding serenely before the squalls.

In a landscape so barren of detail, so empty of anything three hands higher than a duck's beak, it seemed almost unbelievable that such a massive structure should have found its way out here. As I toiled up the slope into the town she continued to work and rework her way through my imagination like the hook of a cheap pop song. A face appeared at a window watching me, her features as indistinct as an old statue's in the tadpoling raindrops. Otherwise the streets were empty as I passed the Pilgrim's Parlour and Ye Olde Tea Shoppe until I came up to the cathedral's front door. If anything she was even more impressive close up and my back arched as I gazed up in simple wonder at the black cascading stonework.

This magnificent monastery was founded by Saint Etheldreda, Queen of Northumbria, in 673 A.D. She was a strange and beautiful queen of ice and flame, a woman of legendary unselfishness endowed with the gift of prophecy. She never washed in warm water and prayed from midnight until dawn. Even when terminally ill she delighted in the painful swellings which tormented her. But the most unusual aspect of her quirky character was that she did not believe in sex either before or after marriage. Despite two husbands, she remained a virgin and it was on this frigid reputation that her cult – and the cathedral – were built.

After the death of her first husband, Tondbert, a Fen prince, she came to Ely to devote her life to prayer. Five years later her father forced her to marry Egfrith, son of Oswy, King of Northumbria. He too made unreasonable demands on Etheldreda's body and at one stage complete with army he chased her right across Northumbria. She took refuge on a promontory and her virginity was saved by a week of storms which so discouraged the damp and sad Egfrith that he fully and finally gave up on her.

It is a singular story, vivid with threats of violence and thwarted lusts and yet, just by stooping through the small wooden door of the cathedral and looking up and around at the awesome size of the brooding, pillared nave, I could immediately sense something of the ice queen's personality. The huge, dark-streaked spaces and high arches do not tell of the human failings of us ordinary people but the vast, intangible mystery of God. There was not a trace of sensuality in that flagstoned floor, neither was there any warmth in the chilling gusts of wind.

I moved past two people keeping warm next to a rumbling stove. Looking up again, my breath kept failing me, whether from feelings of fear or love I could not be quite sure. *My house is very big and you are very little*, those flaking walls told me. *I am very old and you are very young. You are in Etheldreda's house. Keep off the grass.*

Her shrine, like so much else that was holy, was broken up in the Reformation. Moving closer to the altar, I stood under the Lantern Tower and it engulfed me again – this sense of mystery and wonder – as I looked up at the shafts of hard, stellar light bursting in through the windows and coming together in a shimmering white starburst in the shadows of the distant rafters.

Just near the Lady Chapel I met Canon Murray McDonald, a precise cleric with an accent woodsmoked by public school. He explained that this was the mother church of the diocese of Ely; throughout the year they had some hundred thousand visitors. Three pilgrimages a week came from East Anglia; people were encouraged to concentrate on a part of the cathedral, study it and try to decide what it was saying to them.

He told me a bit about Etheldreda too, of how she was popularly known as Audrey and of the medieval fairs which were held in her honour on the seventeenth day of October. At such fairs, cheap trumpery – jewellery and such-like – would be sold. This was identified as 'St Audrey' stuff, hence the modern word which came from this, tawdry.

I cycled back into the town and found a room in the White Hart Hotel, a most curious place full of sloping floorboards and a passageway festooned with plastic flowers. There was a dog who went berserk with rage at the sight of a visitor and someone who seemed to be living rough on the floor of the residents' lounge.

It was dusk and the rain had stopped when I went back to the cathedral again, walking down past the school and the dean's house where the silhouettes of people moved, black on gold, in the rooms' light. From somewhere deep in the darkness came the sound of choir practice. All around the cathedral grounds birds flitted past the spiky parapets and chipped gargoyles. The taste of newly mown grass hung in the damp air.

Wandering again around the cold, shadowy interior, trying to second-guess the real nature of the place, I saw the urgent appeals for cash, the notices that all but commanded the visitor to donate a pound, the demands for more money for the use of a camera, the tourists milling about who would be hard pushed to tell the difference between a prayer and a poke in the eye. Etheldreda's house was in dire physical distress. On the notice-board I read that the stonework in the east end of the cathedral was in need of repair, the gable of the south transept had to be rebuilt. There were no financial reserves.

Here was a church floundering towards an honourable grave, one which, despite its abundant beauty, had not escaped the sickness of the modern church. In the mad days of the Reformation people cared enough about these places to knock them down. Now they were being killed by the even deadlier attack of spiritual syphilis, and were fast becoming crumbling tourist shrines, bowed down by the cobwebs of penury; huge monuments to the modern death of holiness.

The quest for the purpose and meaning of holiness was at the heart of my pilgrimages during that year of 1984. I wanted to find out what it meant and if it still existed in the land. I wanted to define its characteristics and establish the dispositions of this word from the Anglo-Saxon *halig*; something which must be kept complete or inviolable; something which was one or whole; something which was of high moral excellence, spiritually perfect, of God.

This building had clearly grown out of a sense of holiness; out of something spiritually perfect which had once existed in the soul of man who then created it to mirror that something. It had been built on that which was complete, inviolate, one or whole. Yet the noticeboard told you that it was far from complete now. It was incomplete, violated. Could God still reside in this house where cameras flashed and damp winds blew around urgent appeals for yet more cash?

The Lady Chapel was a bright exception to the rest of the building; a warm place, generous in its proportions and glimmering with lots of cheerful windows. It was in there I bumped into a man with the beefy arms of a labourer who turned out to be a musician. He was blowing down a large tin funnel and listening to the sound. 'An organ would sound lovely in this chapel,' he announced.

'So what does it sound like in the cathedral?' I asked.

'It sounds lovely in there too. It's the way you play it, you know. You can make almost anything sound lovely if you know how to play it. But most musicians are bombastic. That's the trouble these days. Bombasticism. That's why so many organs sound so awful.'

He piped on his funnel a few more times, nodded to himself and left.

The next day, Good Friday, I went to the morning service in the cathedral. It was the coldest service I have ever attended. At first I found only one lady sitting in front of the altar and asked her if it was just she and me but she said she thought there was a service going on somewhere in the choir stalls. I picked my way around scaffolding draped in polythene sheets and found about a hundred and fifty people shivering in the choir stalls. Staccato gusts of wind jabbed about in the roof and thumped against the polythene. The badly adjusted microphone made the disembodied voice echo like announcements in a railway station: 'We nonowowow turnturnturn . . .' All the choirboys were wearing gloves. Most of the congregation resembled dummies in the window of an Oxfam shop with their scarves, grey overcoats and odd glimpses of thick flannelled ankles.

Even that great hymn 'When I Survey the Wondrous Cross' failed to lift the cold. I was shivering so much I could not later understand much of my notes on Canon McDonald's sermon. I think it went something like this:

'At the heart of the gospel there is not a dream but an event, an act that took place in the world. When Jesus shouted that it was finished it was the act of a man who had climbed a mountain and cried in delight that he had made it. The goal has been reached. Nothing more can be done. No more can be added. His death is perfect. There is no more you can say. Here you see God's word for man. The height and the depth. The dreadful evil that is man also. The truth about ourselves. He bowed his head and gave up his spirit. Part of that perfection is faith and trust. In death, Jesus surrenders himself to God and gives himself to you. This is the mystery that Paul so often leads us to. We come not to mourn the passing of the Lord but to receive life. We come to catch the meaning of life. So this is an event in which we are baptized in Christ Jesus.'

The canon's bleak, pithy sentences seemed of a piece with the place; of a piece with the scaffolding and the polythene; of a piece with the bone-crushing cold and the way that the normal ornate silver cross on the altar had been replaced by a wooden cross so that we would remember the original one, rough-hewn and full of splinters. Everything about the service had been so taut and shorn of anything that might cheer and comfort us it might even have pleased old Etheldreda herself, might even have put a smile on the beautiful, serious lips of that ice queen whose cold, autocratic eye clearly still watches over the building.

Afterwards I jumped on my bike and cycled down to the river where two swans, their necks like great white question marks, were swimming together near a marina called Babylon. A man poked his head out of a hatch and shouted something at me. I later nosed around a cemetery where I found a huge mountain of flowers, all dead and rotten except for some giant white lilies. So what was the secret of the lilies? The secret of the lilies, it turned out on closer inspection, was that they were plastic.

The rain was sheeting down as I struggled against the icy shotgun blasts of the Fen blows along the road to Downham Market. Pylons trooped through the rain mists and, in the ditches, pampas grass with forlorn black beards whipped the winds. I picked up that mysterious trail of carrots again and came across numerous corpses of flattened frogs. It was still spring. It was still the time of mass migrations and the endless fornication of frogs.

It was the steady northerly wind that was the greatest cause of my misery and I recalled that old Gaelic blessing:

> May the roads rise with you
> And the winds always be at your back
> And may the Lord hold you in the hollow of his hand.

No winds at my back out here. Just a steady pounding against my face and chest like some enraged boxer ready and willing to flail away forever. Just a recurring sense of misery that I was away from home and new baby, out in the freezing rain, depressed with the sheer unendurable effort of starting a new book, hardly able to understand what I was up to or what I might find out. Yet again.

Ely Cathedral was still haunting parts of my mind, still rearing up and over me like some enfolding nightmare from which there was no awakening. The pillars and shimmering tower of light had come back to me in a series of dissolving dreams, almost as if Etheldreda was trying to say something about herself as I turned my back on her, almost as if she was pointing out that I had made a very big mistake indeed in writing off her great house as a cobwebbed tourist shrine.

*You do not understand the allure of the ice queen of the Fens then? You do not understand that there is life as well as death in my house? Never forget that like the scorpion I can still lash out and sting you dead. Never forget that I reign over ice.*

These mute naggings came to me in wordless, slightly corrosive questions. Was Etheldreda out there in those great billowing rain clouds? Was it her power over ice that was making my hands turn red-raw and my face sting with the cold? Was it her hands that were clutching at my throat and making my chest ache with pain? Two lorries roared past me, sending buckets of rain over me and making me stop to get off my bike, head bowed low and bones frozen to the marrow, crying out loud for her to just leave me alone.

The rain stopped for a while and I got back on my bike. Occasionally I spotted the odd farmer going about his work, his farmyard jobs as hard and elemental as the land itself which, together with all these swirling skies, dictated the very rhythm of the Fen days.

The road was curiously empty for this time of year – just the odd car and certainly no one on foot or bicycle. In medieval times, Easter on the road to Walsingham would have presented a very different picture: gripped by fantastic religious spasms, whole armies of people would have been moving along this road at this, the beginning of the pilgrimage season. The scene is easy to imagine. There would be pilgrims living by alms, mendicants and friars, labourers revolting against the bonds of the soil and minstrels out to soothe the blistered and weary with their songs. There would be quacks telling of cures for the kiss of vipers and drug-sellers with balms for piles and worms. Peasants out of bond would be scurrying along with falconers and mummers. Tumblers would mix with pardoners selling indulgences which gave time off in hell. And sprinkled through all these would be a whole rabble of clippers of coin, robbers crouching in coppice or ditch, bear-baiters, shipmen pretending losses at sea and singers of bawdy songs.

They would have been on a ceaseless ramble with their screaming children and creaking carts; some seeking to honour vows made in illness and others wanting to square the debt of a terrible sin; some enjoying the merriment of the road and others merely wanting to get up the nose of the king. But whatever their individual motives they all, in their own ways, were brought together in one common act of pilgrimage insofar as they were all seeking out the guiding, healing, protecting powers of God.

But this morning, with the land all around waiting for the first reviving kiss of summer, no one was going anywhere. Down on the junction to the road to Downham Market a gypsy caravan stood on a grass verge surrounded by a couple of clapped-out cars and a small mountain of dead washing machines.

My left knee was beginning to swell up and give me a lot of pain that afternoon as I cycled past empty fields towards King's Lynn. Everything seemed banged down by a great fist of grey; rain clouds were piling up on the horizon again. I passed a bricked-up chapel. Was Etheldreda still around and escorting me off the property? Just then something huge and flashily bright began twisting around in the middle of the rain clouds.

It turned the banks from black to grey to yellow and then the winds began shunting everything in sight. Lo and behold there appeared a massive shimmer of sun; a sort of golden downpour came swarming through a big blue gap in the lightening clouds, singing a hymn of renewal as it drenched everything with a brilliant warmth.

I freewheeled down a hill and passed under an arch of the old walled ramparts of King's Lynn, the sunshine rolling bright golden hoops along the curving streets, dancing up against the shop windows and leaping from rooftop to rooftop, making the whole town glitter like something magical as promises of the coming summer were whispered down every lane and around every corner.

King's Lynn is an important centre for pilgrimage since it was here, on the mouth of the river Ouse, that many thousands of pilgrims from overseas embarked *en route* to Walsingham. It still has its own wayside chapel where pilgrims would stop to offer up prayers for a safe journey, and it was the home of Margery Kempe, a nutty mystic whose extraordinary life, back in the fourteenth century, was in itself one long pilgrimage which she wrote about in *The Book of Margery Kempe*. She visited Canterbury and Compostela and even accomplished the Holy Grail of every pilgrim: a visit to the Holy Land itself at a time when it was an extremely arduous journey involving taking a ship from Italy to Damietta in Egypt then travelling by camel across the Sinai desert to Jerusalem before coming back by way of Crete, Cyprus or Rome.

A proto-feminist who frequently made life difficult for any men in her vicinity, Margery Kempe had a great shout of joy in her personality. She could also be a pain in the neck. One contemporary wrote: 'A prolonged and violent shriek broke from her lips at the sight of anything holy.'

I passed her birthplace, gulls wheeling overhead, laughing their thin, rackety cries as I searched for a bed. A lot is made of the beauty of King's Lynn – usually by those from King's Lynn – but I could not see it. Some of the streets, it is true, drip with a medieval charm but there is too much of the new packed cheek by jowl with the old. Warehouses rub shoulders with old churches. Factories brush up against cobbled squares. The place does not seem to have a coherent personality, a little like Margery Kempe, perhaps.

The next morning I cycled out past the wire fences of an industrial estate on the outskirts of the town and, quite soon, picked up that mysterious line of half-eaten carrots again. After the ironed flatness of the Fens, the land out here rolled and sloped in an emphatic way, the fields dotted with cows and fenced around by meandering hawthorn hedges which rattled in the breeze.

The swelling in my knee had gone down and, for the first time since I had left home, I was beginning to feel quite chirpy. Old Celtic beliefs taught that, on Easter Day, the sun always danced for joy. Well, the sun was not exactly dancing with joy but she was certainly winking down through the clouds in great good humour as I bowled along towards Walsingham.

The gardens were bursting with the first emblems of spring – the delicate yellow avalanches of forsythia, the perfumed curls of the hyacinth and the first pink shivers of blossom on the trees. So what better time to travel to Walsingham, one of the greatest shrines in all Christendom, to celebrate the death and resurrection of the Lord?

Walsingham attracts 250,000 pilgrims a year with 30,000 of them staying overnight. My first impression, when I coasted down into the village square, was that they had all decided to pitch up on the same day. The tiny streets were jam-packed with pilgrims, all wearing their widest smiles and promenading arm in arm. They gathered on every corner and hung on every lamp-post while nuns skittered through them with their elbows flashing and shoulders jerking back and forth in the I've-got-work-to-do-even-if-you-haven't way that nuns often have.

I signed into the Pilgrim Centre – a positive beehive of fire doors and spartan dormitories – and soon discovered that the main cause of my impression of a place about to burst under the weight of its own jollity was Student Cross: a crowd of more than two hundred students of doubtful sanity who, as part of the Easter celebration, had formed into groups from Nottingham, Leicester, Kettering, Oxford, Colchester and London and *walked* to Walsingham on a journey lasting seven days, each group carrying a life-size wooden cross.

It appeared that the people of Norfolk always knew that Easter had begun when they spotted such hymn-singing gangs stumbling past their doors as they shouldered their great crosses over the landscape. Even in the pouring rain it was said to be an extraordinarily uplifting sight as they trooped down into Walsingham, sodden and yet still singing, taking it in turns to carry the cross a few more yards towards their goal.

I located some in a café where they were all sprawled around a single cup of tea, many with their arms around one another. They treated their journey, they explained, as a sort of walking retreat, a period of suffering and denial, a sharing of insights and bidding prayers, ending up in a time of joyful celebration here in Walsingham.

After a service in the morning they set off to cover some twenty miles a day, resting at various stations when they might hear a talk from the local vicar or, as on last Maundy Thursday, have their feet washed by chaplains. After a few hours in a pub they slept – died? – on the floors of the church halls. 'We like to get through about eight pints a day or a firkin a week,' one offered. 'Beer keeps you going.'

Pilgrimage being a communal activity they often flung their arms around one another for a huge cuddle and a lot of shouting. They might massage one another's feet or legs or merely sit around fondling one another's knees. This was called a grundle. 'Grundles are a great help keeping us on the road,' said Marion Taylor, a black-eyed student from London. 'And there's nothing at all sexual about them.'

That evening a gang of us trooped the mile or so out of Walsingham for a communion service in the Chapel of

Reconciliation, the new Catholic church built next to the old pilgrim Slipper Chapel. It was a warm, dark night, full with the sounds of a chuckling river and creaking tree trunks. Bare branches waved over our heads like poised whips and something small, black and squealing dashed across the road in front of us.

Millions of stars were smashed across the sky like vast scatterings of powdered glass. The Milky Way was once known as Walsingham Way – partly because it became associated with Our Lady's milk and also because it illuminated the lanes and directed the pilgrims journeying here.

I left the group and went into the Slipper Chapel alone. It was stone-built with a few pews and a prayer on the altar: 'That we may be one.' Next to the altar was a glimmering bank of votive candles, shivering bright in the draught and with curling wisps of black smoke. Candle flames are very evocative. They continue our prayers. There is something deeply pure in the tiny heart of those yellow flames, something which draws you to them. You ponder on the souls of all those millions of pilgrims who have come and gone; all those who have lit candles here before taking off their shoes and walking the last mile to the village, all beautiful with prayerful hearts.

A German choir, dressed in smart blue coats and dicky bows, joined us for the communion service in the Chapel of Reconciliation, with its modern circular structure of red brick and polished wood. It turned out to be one of those beautiful services that makes your heart go hang-gliding and you wish would go on forever. Their guide, a Welshman, read from St Paul's letter to the Colossians. The German choir sang their hymns of love with a blissful relish and clearly inspired by them we all followed their lead, weaving our harmonies with their harmonies until one suspected the very walls might collapse before the swelling beauty of our song.

'One of the most telling evidences of the truth of the resurrection is the change of the attitude of the apostles,' said the preacher. 'They went from gloom to despair to overwhelming hope. The resurrection of Jesus brings us living hope. The Lord

has risen and lives forever. The Lord came to give us life.
Christians ought to be the most joyful as we live in hope of the
resurrection.'

Everyone was invited to embrace and shake hands before taking communion. 'It is a matter of regret,' said one priest, 'that
we are forbidden by law to give communion to any other than
Catholics.'

It was the one sour note in a sublime evening. Here we all
were, at a time when unity was at the heart of most prayers, in
a village where Anglican and Catholic leaders had taken thousands of followers to each other's shrines, in a building where
a congregation had worshipped beautifully together and still
the black lunatic hand of a centuries-old schism was hanging
over us.

All any sane Christian wants is to kneel together before one
cross but still there are Church leaders, with their doctrinal
blinkers and tuppenny ha'penny visions, determined we should
stay apart. Even those students who had shouldered crosses to
Walsingham could not now take communion together. A
Church at war with itself is a Church at war with God. A
Church which fails to live together will die apart.

There and then I resolved to take communion wherever it
became available. No one was going to produce a lie detector
before giving me the wafer and the wine and in this way I was
going to become my own tiny instrument of the Church's
healing.

And so it turned out as I spent the rest of that summer bum-
bling around the country taking communion from hands
young and hands gnarled; sipping wine sweet and wine sour;
listening to benedictions soft and benedictions harsh; enjoying
my own prayer life on the pilgrim road without getting angry
and bogged down in the dog days of some old bishop's bigotry.

## 2

## 'Half Church of God,
## Half Castle 'Gainst the Scots'

------◆------

ESCOMB · BAMBURGH · LINDISFARNE

It was still early in the morning but already the sun was boiling the brains out of the land as our coach swept through the Durham countryside. Bright puffs of poppies stood in the young silky green corn with the massed trumpets of the giant hogweed on the bank of a burn. Gravel pinged on the metal underbelly of the coach and its engine roared lustily as the driver changed down before turning corner after corner.

We swept through yet another of those perfect Durhamshire stone villages where children were playing hop-scotch near an old church and a pair of naked feet were poking out of a window. What magical places these villages were with names that tugged at the heart like Spennymoor, Seldom Seen and Pity Me.

All week we had raced over sprawling moors and past pigeon lofts and allotments; we had climbed over ruined castles and been told tales of the giant Lambton worm; we had 'click' stops to photograph mournful Gothic ruins and coffee stops in damp villages where fluorescent bingo halls sat next to gilded curry palaces.

Everywhere the summer had begun to burst up out of the land, making the weeds and nettles come charging up out of the industrial litter of abandoned factories, sending cartwheels of sunshine rolling over the stepped mounds of the open-cast mines, dragging out the first leaves of the trees, energizing the very soil and making everything as lusty as a new-born baby.

Today, the sixth day of our pilgrimage around the holy spots of North England, we were going to Lindisfarne, Holy Island, tucked right up in the north-east corner. The gears growled low and loud again as the coach toiled up a savage slope.

We had gathered the previous Sunday at Durham University, an unlikely collection of pilgrims for the most part. There were touches of the shires and the odd whiff of the holiday camp. We were not too poor nor too rich but mostly we seemed reasonably well educated. For the most part we had silver hair, thick legs and varicose veins. We wore sensible clothes with flat leather shoes. Now that we had lost the self-absorbed vanity of youth, we understood that beauty was but a temporary gift which would soon fade. There was the odd gash of lipstick and the perfume was dabbed on the neck, more to create a noise than an alluring scent. We had put all that nonsense aside now.

We took our photographs with cheap cameras and were forever telling little stories and laughing a lot unless someone tried to pinch our allotted seat on the coach when our laughter froze and we stamped our feet and became very serious indeed.

We had a fair bit of religious conviction too and lots of us whiled away happy moments studying the shape of the church rafters or going down on our knees in prayer at the altar of some small Saxon church, mindful of the continuity of prayer of many thousands of people over the centuries. We were a mellow bunch, not given to postures, calm as people often are in the autumn of their lives, ready for what was to come, a lot of us hopeful we would be returning to the arms of the loved ones we had buried years earlier.

Yes, that was about the way we were on that bus. We were happy and easy in our stained glass hours. We wanted to go, if that was all right, but we would stay if it wasn't. We just didn't want to make any sort of fuss.

Our first stop of the week had been at Escomb to visit the Saxon church there, one of the oldest in Britain. Sunshine streamed through the yew leaves in the graveyard and the air was abuzz with midges and the thwack of tennis balls. Just near the porch I found a gravestone with a carving of a man smiling his head off on it. I told Jenny I liked that very much and rather hoped to have something like that on mine. 'All things duly considered,' I wanted written on my tombstone, 'I would rather be down here than watching television.'

We also found gravestones with the skull and crossbones on them. Jo explained that the skull and crossbones were traditionally supposed to show the death had been by plague or even that they had been robbers or pirates. This was not so. The skull and crossbones, she said, were believed to be the minimum Gabriel needed to fix up a decent resurrection; they were the very symbol of hope to medieval people and were only later taken up by pirates. Jo knew everything and it was to her we always turned when we needed something explained.

It was in the graveyard I first noticed Walter examining the trees. His wife had levered him out of his own garden for this trip so, while others looked at old churchy things, he mooched about examining trees and shrubs, pulling the foliage to one side and feeling their stems before nodding, satisfied, and, more often than not, taking his pipe out of his mouth and letting fall a long stream of spit.

Escomb church itself was a sparse, witty structure in mismatching stones taken from the ruins of a local Roman fort. A sundial hung on the wall outside with just three lines on it suggesting, said Jo, that the monks were more concerned with the times of prayer than the exact hour of day. Inside the church had the shorn piety of the age of Bede; a simple whitewashed elegance with a spray of lilies next to the font. There were no windows on the north wall, the devil's wall, and during christenings the door was always left open to let the devil out. You could tell the church was still deeply cherished from the polished pews and spotless stone floors. 'I love things that have been looked after,' said Pat. 'To me that's lovely.'

Today, on our journey to Lindisfarne, the sun was still climbing steadily up the back of the bluest sky. Gaudy lines of shivering lupins were marching down through the gardens of the old cottages, some smothered with roses and clematis.

The chatter was continuing and I again noted how incredibly well-travelled we all were; how the conversation swung easily from the tulip fields of Holland to package tours of the Rhine; how Venice was full of rip-off merchants and how they often charged an extra pound just to sit outside and drink a cup of coffee. One spoke of the incredible cost of toilets in Capri and how her husband had always promised to buy her a black frock and a toilet in Capri for her retirement. Madge recalled how difficult it was to climb the spire of Canterbury Cathedral while Jo had even been to Egypt but had found it 'hot and tiring' so she was going to stick to good old England from now on.

We were on a charter with Tate's Travel, 29 of us – 19 women and 10 men – now going at 50 miles an hour up a tarmacadam road with everyone laughing their socks off and coming to the village of Felton. 'The sweet william flower came from here,' our driver said over the microphone. 'It was here that William gathered forces against the Scots under Bonnie Prince Charlie. Thereafter, in Scotland, the same flower was called the stinking billy.'

Everywhere we travelled we heard of the centuries-old quarrel between the English and the Scots. The tartan terrors had spread such fear they even prompted the Romans to build Hadrian's Wall to keep them out; in later years, an order came down that 'all havens should be fenced with bulwarks and bloke houses against the Scots.' Churches had to double up as fortresses in which the women and cattle could be hidden when the boys came down intent on a spot of looting and raping. Some of them still had their arrow slits.

In Chester-le-Street, we were told that, until recently, there had been a ball game in which the whole village had taken part, kicking one ball around, stemming from the time when knights had kicked around the heads of Scottish invaders. Sir Walter Scott had described Durham as 'Half Church of God, half castle 'gainst the Scots'.

We had another 'click' stop at Walworth Castle – 'painted by Turner and written about by Shakespeare', said our driver – before driving on past sloping fields and a languid sea. Just off the coast sat the Farne Islands, dull brown in drifting white, immobile in the plashy waves, as mysterious as the sea mists that enshrouded them. A flock of oyster-catchers wheeled overhead, their beaks shrieking with bad news as their bellies glinted as if on fire in the still rising sun. A water tower sat on the horizon like a giant black mushroom. It was going to be a boiler for certain although way out on the horizon some grey-black clouds were piling up with the promise of a few cooling spits.

The lunch stop was in Bamburgh. Even before the driver had switched off the ignition many of us were already standing up in the aisle wanting to stomp up the hill 'to do' the castle before eating. It was extraordinary, I thought, the way some so old become so young again; the way they were happy to tackle the biggest slopes while the rest of us were rather more content to stick to the flatlands and quiet little hobbles, sucking a lollipop. We weren't all bursting with energy. The hardcore always waited for the rest to get off the bus before they stood up.

'What I've always said is never stand up if you can sit down,' said Stan. 'And never sit down when you can lie down.'

Even as we alighted I noticed again we did not cohere as a group; no one stood around waiting for someone else to take the lead. The whole lot split up immediately like a school class dismissed at the end of the day, with each person chasing off after whatever pleased them. This decisive independence had been born out of long periods of loneliness, perhaps, since I was certain that a lot of us were lonely. The young cover up their loneliness with endless chatter and jungle music but, sometimes, I caught one of our lot standing in the corner of a graveyard, dusting an invisible tear away from the corner of her eye with a fingertip as her body was mauled by a lovely memory, perhaps, of a time hand in hand with a loved one.

There were couples, of course, like Danny and Anne or Walter and Pat. I must say I know of nothing more fabulous – in an age when relationships everywhere are fracturing – than following Walter and Pat, with some 160 years between the two of them, as I did that day in Bamburgh, as they tootled along the pavement, arm in arm, quietly fussing over one another.

'Ee Walter I do hope they've got some real milk with the tea in this café.'

'They'll have some, lass. Stop worrying will you?'

'It's daft, I know, but I just can't drink tea without real milk.'

Some went straight into the café but most of us wandered on up the road to St Aidan's Church, the site of the death of Aidan, the stag, the first apostle of Christianity in England. The shadows of those great saints of old fell across my path again and again that year. In Aidan's story we have the perfect example of one such man, ushered into a confused age by God to set up a communion of saints and an age of scholarship and, in so doing, to save the world at a time when Rome had fallen and all certainties had broken apart.

Aidan was first sent here from the island of Iona by St Columba, and the Northumbrian king, King Oswald, made him the first bishop of Lindisfarne. From this island retreat he journeyed on foot, far and wide through Northumbria, across marsh and meadow, often through thorns and stones, everywhere reciting psalms, reading the Bible and preaching the wild word of God.

A model of moral probity, his method was to teach by the example of his gentleness and goodness, by the sacrifice of all luxury. He preached into the teeth of a hurricane of Danish violence and his mission was to heal. King Oswald died and the next king, King Oswin, gave Aidan a fine horse to travel on. Aidan immediately gave it to a beggar. The infuriated king asked him if he could not find a less valuable horse to give away but Aidan merely replied by asking the king if a child of a mare was more important than a child of God. Nevertheless the two became great friends and, when the king was murdered, Aidan died of a broken heart here, in Bamburgh, twelve days later.

It had been a glorious summer day, rather like this one, when he died but that night the sky turned black at the edges and there was a wild fury in it. A great beam of light shone down through the fury and a crowd of angels climbed down it, as if it were a ladder. At the foot of the ladder the angels picked up Aidan's soul and carried it up to heaven. This great metaphysical funeral was witnessed, in a vision, by a 17-year-old boy who had been out looking after his sheep in the low hills that night. He went straight to the nearest monastery at Melrose – a sister house of Lindisfarne – and became a monk. Which was how, in 651, St Cuthbert entered our journey.

After Bamburgh the land became flatter with sparse lonely trees, hunched down against the bitter North Sea winds, when I caught sight of Lindisfarne castle, vivid and alluring, poking up above the sunken contours of the distant seascape. It disappeared and came back again, a big and bold sort of fairy castle with sharp black lines which sprang out of the rock in such a way that the castle and rock seemed one and the same. We turned off the main road and down a cow parsleyed lane where there were curling trails of tractors in the young green corn. A chattering helicopter was sweeping back and forth spraying the crops.

Big black-faced gulls swooped overhead when we came down to the causeway and the road which was to take us to the island. This causeway always has an enchantment about it – especially when you are part of a group of fellow pilgrims. I had gone back to that spot three times that year and the aspect never ceased to amaze, not because of its spectacular view but because of its clear promise of holiness. It was here I made my first real discovery about holiness since such islands have it in abundance, which is why those saints of old sought out such places.

Islands mediate the concept of holiness to us. They are one, whole, apart. They are places of pure solitude where man alone may seek out and attempt to understand the nature of the mystery. The sea all around is the very material of God – the way of baptism, regeneration and faith; the waters in which we must be born again. To such islands the soul might return at the end of life.

Yes, there's a powerful, dreaming holiness around Lindisfarne. It drifts through the great sea winds, through those wide stretches of sand dotted by pools and curling mounds of lugworm. You can hear it even in the fluting calls of the sandpipers, in the flapping wings of the stork pinning a beautiful arc of flight against a clear sky and the low distant roar of the incoming tide.

But, most of all, holiness is not suggested by a great edifice which has taken thousands of years and thousands of lives to build. Here, on Lindisfarne, it is etched across our minds by the line of old broken sticks stretching across the sands to mark out Pilgrim's Way. Holiness is always best expressed by the simple, the humble and the poor. And here those sticks sing a song of holiness to the sea winds; they surround the journeying pilgrim with the very music of the Cross as he makes his way across the softly sinking sand to Holy Island itself.

Even in the pouring rain the island can look ravishing, though that day it looked particularly magical. The sun burnished the huge pools dotted around the causeway, goslings moved through fiery yellow pools as children on the other side tumbled down the slopes of the sand dunes. About a dozen people were following the broken sticks of Pilgrim's Way.

The village itself was a sprawling, stone jumble, gathered around post office and pub, pegged out between the priory ruins on one side and the bay road to the castle on the other. A large stone cross stood in the square where a pack of clean and scrubbed wolf cubs were sitting together eating sandwiches on the grass.

The priory was a rubble with a few walls and one big arch still intact. A few of us tagged along behind a guide who said the local people were so keen on honouring the saints of old they bought all the red sandstone and built the priory out of nothing. 'Up here is what's left of a flying buttress.'

'What's that? Some sort of butterfly is it?'

We saw the dining area where the old monks would have eaten. We know they ate no meat, drank no ale and refused anything with dripping or seasoning. The remains of another room showed a stone-lined pit where they salted food. It must have been a life shorn of any kind of comfort, maintaining the rounds of work and worship, conducting the long night vigils, teaching by their perfect example, exalting Christ and crucifying selves.

But of all the old saints here it was Cuthbert who was the most vivid. His silver tongue could wreak havoc, even in the imagination of birds. In common with many other saints, Cuthbert had a marvellous relationship with the animal kingdom, once reprimanding a flock of crows who kept pinching the priory's barley and even once telling off some others for taking the thatch from his house. When they still did it he banished them from the island until they came sneaking back, muttering apologies.

Once, when hungry in the wilderness, an eagle dropped a fish for Cuthbert to eat. He was particularly fond of the eider duck – still known as St Cuthbert's ducklings. It was sometimes his practice to stand in the sea all night praising God, and often in the mornings, when he had finished his prayers, seals would come out of the water to dry his feet and breathe on them to restore the warmth.

A specialist in personal holiness, he was also a terrific preacher with the gift of healing. Bede, the chronicler of those times, repeatedly referred to him as the 'child of God', and once Cuthbert healed a woman's dying baby with a kiss. When he became prior of Lindisfarne he had to wean the monks off Druidism, instituting prayer as the main weapon against evil. But he always longed for the solitary life and, after twelve years at Lindisfarne, he went to live as a hermit in a small, rough cell on the Farne Islands. He died in prayer there on March 20, 687. Lighted flares told of his death and monks brought his body back here to rest.

The main church on Lindisfarne was the parish church of St Mary, a fine mish-mash of the original and restored. It had a beautiful carpet on the altar which reproduced a page of the famous Lindisfarne Gospels, now in the British Museum, which were written with quills, soot, glue and water. The church had a fine, cosy porch too – most important in any church since it was here that all services began; here where we were supposed to begin our communion with God and his angels. Or so Jo said.

Later a few of us walked out past the bay down to the castle. The bay itself had the confident sweep of a tropical lagoon, dotted with many strange upturned fishing boats used as sheds. Lots of kids were messing about in the rock pools. Some of our group had gone straight to the bay front benches to sit, legs apart and hands dangling between knees, and gaze out at the riffling waves.

The castle – now owned by the National Trust – was an enchanting place with small cosy rooms and long galleries, all largely built of stone from the priory when it was knocked down in the Dissolution, as yet another fortification against the marauding Scots. Out on the battery there was a fine view from Berwick-on-Tweed in the North to Bamburgh in the South. Islands were scattered haphazardly over the sea and Lindisfarne was spread out at my feet, as bright and glittery as a cheap fire-work in all this sunlight, a magical little kingdom of criss-crossing dry-stone walls, ruined priory and petrel-haunted crags. Just across a channel were sandbanks and mudflats with two strange obelisks on one island, put there as navigational aids for ships at the turn of the century coming in to pick up consignments of lime.

When we got back to the car park at the appointed time, a few of us had gone missing yet again and the driver was worried we would be stranded on the island by the incoming tide. 'These old 'uns can be a reet pain in the neck,' he moaned. 'They go off into fields and have a snooze and it takes ages to find them. No idea of time they've got.'

We drove off the island with the sun dipping down towards the trees and throwing long shadows over the road. A man was out in his garden spraying a lot of tiny rainbows into his plants. Down in Alnwick we paused to admire the strange mock figures on the castle battlements, later slowing to walking pace to drive through the stone arch on the main street. 'Tuck your elbows in,' said the driver. 'Better still, close your eyes 'cos that's what I'll be doing.'

This was the last day of our pilgrimage together and as we roared southwards I closed my eyes and thought of the week and its shifts of mood; of those who had been travelling with us; of the quiet and noisy; of the deaf and ebullient; of the prayerful and the atheistic; of the lonely and the merely pathetic. We had explored some glorious ruins together and seen enchanting churches, but of all we had heard about and seen that week, there was little that matched up to the magnificence of Durham Cathedral, whose great shadow had fallen right over us like a blessing from the angel Gabriel himself.

We had gathered inside the cathedral early in the morning to be shown around by one of the vergers. It would be good to get in there early, we'd been warned, because the guides were still fresh. I suspect this one was still fresh when he went to bed since he was the sort of man Augustine might have described as a hallelujah on two legs, clearly mad about the place and lifting the enthusiastic level of his words way above the normal turgid trudge of guidebooks as he waved his finger here and there, pointing out the massive stone pillars, the ribbed vaults and the great crowning glory of the nave. 'The rock of faith stands here at Durham,' he said at the outset. 'Stand still and look and study. Ask yourself how it came to survive in the modern world. Remember that architecture is but history written in stone.'

We shuffled after this font of odd facts and learned that the bishop's throne here was the highest in Christendom; that the organist had a closed-circuit television to see what was going on in the services and that there were 20 boys in the choir. Some 60 people were employed to work here and, since the building cost half a million a year in maintenance – with £180 a day to heat the place – they had to treat the place as something of a business, making money where they could.

In a year they might get up to a million visitors; only last week they had 800 pilgrims from Sheffield on a chartered train. 'The best time to be here is during the Durham Miners' Gala,' the guide explained, 'even if there are a lot of wonky notes and the smell of beer coming off their brass instruments.'

In the Galilee Chapel we were shown the tomb of the Venerable Bede, the Jarrow monk and father of English history. His most famous work was *The Ecclesiastical History of the English People* which is probably one of the best-selling paperbacks in the history of the world. He also translated parts of the Bible into Anglo Saxon.

It was finally quite moving going to the tomb of Cuthbert himself at the other end of the cathedral; a long plain slab surrounded by high candles with just the name CUTHBERTUS on it. We all stood around silently and looked down at the simple slab as our guide reminded us of the hundreds and thousands of pilgrims who had been there before us, of how bishops had issued indulgences from this spot releasing people from the fear of their sins or penances imposed by a confessor. Here was the very fountainhead of the English faith.

After dinner in the university hall of residence that night I walked back into the old town of Durham, taking a steep path down the road which took me through a wood to the eighteenth-century Prebend's Bridge, a stumpy stone bridge over the river where I lingered awhile as the sun turned the night into a pink bonfire. Even so late the air was still as warm as toast with lovers walking arm in arm along the river banks. Over in the tree-tops on one side was a clamorous row of rooks having a huge bedtime argument, and on the other side of a hurrying weir was a precipitous bank of elm, poplar and beech. And there, right on top of it all, as thrilling as a cavalry charge, rose the gloaming spires of Durham Cathedral, turning from gold to pink to dark brown as the sun bowed out of the day. Just under my feet was the gentle plash of oars, the boat gone from view leaving just the footprints of some giant sculling insect in its wake. Further away again the noises of a rugby game tangled up with the frantic midges. The distant roar of traffic on the next bridge mingled with the strident barking of a dog.

Tired though I was after a long day it was all so perfect; the soaring music of a vivid English summer all being orchestrated in the twilight above a moving river and below a gorgeous cathedral built in the love of the Lord who first built the gorgeous cathedral of the world.

I continued on up the cobbled slopes until I came to the Shakespeare pub where I met a man doing the Australian pools. Wilf Ridley was his name and his job was delivering books to the local prisons – 'They like cowboys, gardening and do-it-yourself books.' He'd also, he said, got a very soft heart which had been broken by a girl. 'I even became a tramp for a bit but gave it up because it was too much like hard work.' He also told me about such legendary characters as Johnny Sixpence and Major Flynn. 'Major Flynn would spend his life going around pubs selling racing tips and stealing people's drinks when they weren't looking. If you bought one of his tips he wrote it on the floor in chalk between your feet. When you read it you were supposed to rub it off with your shoes.'

The curfew bells were tolling when I walked back to the bridge where the deep dark river was still going on its way, glazed orange in parts by the city lights. The flood-lit cathedral was still towering over all and a sense of a beautiful past came seeping out of the night sounds, transforming a tired loneliness into a meditative solitude. I lurched off the bridge and, just by a lamp-post in a splash of orange phosphorescence, spotted a scrunched-up beer can near my feet. I kicked out at it, making it scream with tinny laughter as it bounced across the lane and into the darkness of the wood.

# 3

## Child of the Hebridean Winds

———◆———

GLASGOW · IONA · ST ANDREWS · CARFIN

Deep in the bawling streets of Glasgow where, at midday, there is a bustling pandemonium of shoppers, buskers and cars screaming around corners; where skinny dogs piddle on milk bottles outside grey tenement blocks; where students, who know their Plato from their Aristotle, skirt around pizzas of dried vomit on the pavements; where tiny brown gospel halls are lodged between newsagents and launderettes and where small, bandy-legged men, who seem mounted on invisible elastic and always look drunk – even when they are sober – bounce their ways to seedy pubs . . . deep in all the vivacious shunts of a great city going about her business is the Necropolis, a quiet and still cemetery on a hill next to the cathedral. It was here, one rainy day in June, I began the Celtic leg of my pilgrimage.

Even in the silence of the Necropolis you could learn a lot about Glasgow; of its secret lusts in the used contraceptives scattered inside some of the brooding Gothic tombs; of its problems in the way that many of the tombs had been vandalized; of its weakness for drink in the empty whisky bottles sitting in the bushes; of its energy and contradictions by looking around at the city at your feet – the factories and motorways, hospitals and shipyards all jumbled, cheek by jowl together in one sprawling Hell's Angel of a city who will show anything except the basic tenderness of her heart.

I was sitting in the speckling rain, munching a pear at the base of a stone column with a statue of that great holy ranter,

John Knox, atop it. 'The chief instrument under God of the Reformation in Scotland, died 1572.'

Knox had a natural feeling for the iconoclasm of the Scots and found something deep in their bruising psyche which he could shape and form into furious rebellion. He presented the people with ringing truths wrenched out of the Gospels and brought them together in a tremendous destructive stand against the authority of Imperial London and Catholic Rome. His was the doctrine of personal responsibility: that, in the end, the individual was alone and answerable to God. His was the belief that truth could only be found in scripture: *verbum Dei* – the word of God. His was the affirmation of the simplicity and puritanism of Calvinism, turning to simplicity of worship and away from the stately masked ball of Roman Catholicism.

But, most importantly of all, this Lutheran avenger insisted the people themselves should become the orderers of things. People, he said, could resist, if necessary, by force. By 1560 his people had control of Edinburgh and this fiery man eventually won a prolonged fight with Mary Queen of Scots. The people did indeed become the orderers of things and Knox had laid the Calvinist basis of Scottish spiritual life. It was men like Knox and Luther who became architects of schism and their ideas still live out there in those streets.

And there he was now, standing on his column above my head, his ferocious tongue frozen in stone and his fist held high in angry wrath at the continuing venality of this tough, uncompromising city as she brawls her way through the twentieth century, crucifix in one hand and broken bottle in the other, possibly the ugliest and certainly the most energetic city in Europe.

I threw away my pear stump and it was still spitting with rain as I gazed out over the city and the distant traffic roar. Somehow light rain seemed to suit Glasgow. The thin drizzle was in keeping with the monochrome streets and the high exposed yellow sweeps of the motorways. The damp also blended nicely with the ugly high-rise flats. Out on the horizon the cranes of the Clyde shipyards poked into the swirling rain mists, and to my left was a brewery, its pungent smell damped down – though not extinguished – by the rain. But what could ever look worse than the cathedral just down here with her walls blackened by the city's smoke and her roof a horrible green colour? Green!

St Mungo, the patron saint of Glasgow, can hardly have had this sprawling mess in mind when, all those years ago, he came to a lonely spot called Glasghu in search of peace and quiet. A community soon formed around this man – who used to stand in a stream of ice-cold water when he went through his daily offices – until he finally died in 603 from, it was thought, the shock of sitting in a hot bath.

He actually founded that black and green cathedral, described by some as the finest medieval building in Europe, but, shown around by a kindly Flora Smith, I thought it rather narrow and crabbed with lots of nasty pockmarks on the pillars. These pillars had been bashed about in the Reformation – Knox and his boys again. The place was also excessively gloomy, I thought. In one corner I found a well full of litter and, on the other side, a door riddled with holes.

The crypt where Mungo lies buried had clearly been abandoned by daylight forever. Thick stone pillars stood around in cold, damp shadows. Just being there made you shiver a lot and think about fur coats. But Flora did show me a rather lovely tapestry which explained Glasgow's coat of arms: the tree being the frozen branch with which Mungo kindled a monastery fire; the dead robin he brought back to life; the bell he brought back from Rome and the salmon, with the lost ring in its belly, whose miraculous capture saved the honour of a princess. Flora also pointed out a high wooden gallery in the roof where the tax-collectors went to worship for fear of having the congregation throw missiles at them.

As she was talking one of the cathedral guides went scooting past, angrily berating a man for wearing a hat in a holy place. Later I went over and had a chat with him. He was one of those mystifying Glaswegian midgets with black, brilliantined hair, ramrod-straight back, bandy legs, clear skin and shining black eyes which always seemed to be brimming over with alcohol. The thing about such men, I have long decided, is that it is almost impossible to guess their age; this one turned out to be an astonishing 61 when he could easily have been 21.

The following Sunday I came back with my friend the journalist Anne Johnstone for the morning communion service. We were met by long rows of serious-looking ushers, dressed in the white tie and tails more befitting a posh restaurant in London's West End than a cathedral with a green roof in Glasgow.

We were escorted to our seats on the far side of the aisle to discover this service was specifically for the nurses from the local hospital who were sitting in the pews in phalanxes of starched hats. Suitably enough the sermon was about Florence Nightingale and while it started well enough it soon began winding and curling like a slow-moving stream on a hot summer's day and I found my attention wandering, first to the plump generosity of Anne's hands then to the faces of the nurses; one in particular, with green eyes, which were also looking around for something of interest to focus on. If only I had a penny for every hour I had daydreamed during a boring sermon, thinking of friends past and present, a scene from a film, a line from a book, a little worry about whether I had enough money to buy lunch. I bet no one ever daydreamed when Knox let rip.

The sermon ended and I began studying those burnished and best-suited ushers as they moved around preparing to serve communion. These were the honest burghers of Glasgow, weaned on fat cigars and the finest port. I noted the cold, reptilian eye of a banker. There was the adding machine face of an accountant. The pursed lips of a publisher of academic books. A small cold mouth here, of an undertaker perhaps, trained never to show sadness or mirth. Light blue veins wriggled around beneath the polished forehead of the insurance broker. None seemed to have ravaged whisky noses or faces torn apart by a passionate woman. All were perfectly shaved with skin the colour of old piano keys. The suits fitted like old gloves and the shoes were polished. You had to shield your eyes from the dazzle of their respectability. These were the professionals of Glaswegian commercial life with their exquisite hands and carefully manicured fingernails; men who would make it such a pleasure when they took your money off you. They served communion with all the restraint and quiet grace of a four-star hotel, cloth over arm and waiting with infinite patience as you sipped your wine and passed on the chalice. Then came the wafers. By now the sacred significance of the occasion had been lost on me altogether as I watched them moving around me with all the precision of a drill square.

But those faces! They were such a collection of fine faces – each brilliant with the impress of their professional individuality – they might just have been waiting all their lives for a Rembrandt to come and immortalize them. But they wouldn't have liked it in the end. They couldn't have borne the old master's unflinching truth. They would probably have done what the honest burghers of Amsterdam tried to do – suppress it.

The service ended and, as the ushers trooped out, I was still smitten by their aroma of relentless respectability. I wondered aloud to Anne if she thought they sinned much and, in that laughing cynical way of hers, she said they were probably at it all the time. At what though? What were the dark secrets inside those polished and burnished souls?

Had any of the ushers of Glasgow cathedral ever taken drugs and danced the night away to heart attack rock 'n' roll? Had they ever known what it was like to be broken on the anvil of sexual obsession? Would they ever have stolen to feed a hungry baby? Could any of these men have ever *known* – really known – what it could possibly have been like to lie broken in the gutter with newspapers wrapped around their bodies, looking into the neck of an empty sherry bottle and choking on humiliating despair?

Somehow I doubted it.

The ferry went pounding out of the grey granite fishing town of Oban with sleek white gulls swooping down over the aft deck. Some hovered uncertainly, gabbling their fury as the bolder ones snatched bread out of the trippers' hands. All around us, in the great shivering lagoons, were tiny islands dotted with ruined crofts. Way out in the distance a cormorant was busily diving in the hope of food and further out again the snow-capped peak of Ben Nevis. 'It never gets above nought degrees on the top,' a man said, leaning on the ship's rail.

But that day everything was far above nought degrees. Sunshine was striding down over the mountain, beaming happily like an American missionary in a white linen suit and with a huge black Bible under his arm, come to polish up your rusty soul. Behind me a baby was grizzling thinly above the rumbling of the ship's engine.

I was heading for the isle of Iona, the most holy place in Scotland; a lovely, enchanted place – or so I had been told – which had once been colonized by the Druids and where, later, the Celtic Church had been born, a child of the purest innocence, conceived out of holy wedlock between the sea mists and Hebridean winds. I was travelling to pray to Columba, 'tender in every adversity'.

But first there was the island of Mull to cross, some thirty miles of single track road which meandered over gorse hills and swooped down deep valleys. Even as I sat on the bus I could see Mull was a hymn to desolation where little moved except wind on stone. Looking over the rubbled moors, I could just as well have been travelling across a lunar landscape. There was nowhere to hide or run or even weep. No colour in the land either – just light greys and faint greens with the odd smudge of crimson. We passed a herd of shaggy Highland cattle with their huge, ferocious horns and, later, a working peat bog.

From a distance Iona really did look like something from the pages of myth; shell beaches whiter than the whitest detergent, grey crofts dotted around the harbour, stone crosses and cairns, the ruins of the nunnery and the object of my pilgrimage; the great abbey itself where white doves fluttered around the slate roof.

Even as we crossed the causeway on the ferry out of Fionnphort, with the sun blazing down and a foaming trail of spume in our wake, I knew I would fall in love with the place; knew I would leave a bit of myself behind me on those white sandy shores. Emotions soar and plummet on a journey like this but, on that short ferry ride, I stood there bursting with soaring gratitude that I could make a living of sorts doing this.

The sea all around heaved with belches of brilliance. I had been told that Scottish painters had been obsessed by that Hebridean play of light on water; by the dark greens and purples of the sea bed and that amazing white sand. In all this we could see the colours of holiness again – in the tumbling waves on an isolated shore; in the calls of birds in a wing-flashed sky. I looked up and, suitably enough, saw that the trails of two jets had emblazoned a huge fluffy white cross across the roof of the blue sky.

I walked off the ferry and soon came across the nunnery ruins – piles of ruins made to look tidy by the straight borders of closely cut grass. I could just about make out the nave, the aisle and the Lady Chapel. There really was something serene about those old stones and I thought of the words of that great moralist Dr Johnson. 'The man is little to be envied whose piety would not grow warmer among the ruins of Iona,' he wrote.

The air was still a bucket of warm sunshine and the warbling of doves when I approached the abbey. It is not one of those great churches with a splendid ecclesiastical flourish though there is a certain lithe fitness about the stone cloisters and the granite church itself.

It turned out that a German party from Munich had taken over the abbey that week. They all arrived an hour later – a jolly lot they were too – a beefy and well-fed bunch of pastors, office workers, soldiers, engineers and the retired. The individuals soon began emerging over our first meal together. There was

Fritz Eistman, as blind as Mr Magoo, who on the journey to Iona had got on the wrong ferry out of Oban. But he had mercifully been spotted standing on the bridge of another ship altogether when they were only a few hundred yards out to sea. There was also Gunter Gruner who specialized in asking long questions about obscure spiritual problems and Barbara Schuett – 'I am coming from Munich. I am dreaming of coming to Iona for a long while. I am very happy to peel potatoes.'

Peeling potatoes! Hah! I hadn't known about that one. St Columba, who first founded a community here, was a many-sided figure – politician and patriarch, soldier and saint, animal-lover and a bit of a big mouth. He was also a great ascetic with a weakness for the rough things of life which included abstaining from alcohol, working the land with the rest of the monks and sleeping on a stone pillow.

Clearly the abbey had been built on the foundations of his hair-shirt since hardly had we finished our first meal together than I was out in the kitchen, rushing about and washing up hundreds of dishes with the others in a clatter and bang reminiscent of the Parisian *plongeurs* in George Orwell's *Down and Out in Paris and London*. Neither did it end there. Guests were also expected to lay fires, clean the toilets, wash the floors and prepare the food. They were organized into tightly regimented groups accordingly. The Germans accepted this quasi-military regime with fair good grace but I suspected that, had this been an English party in Germany, everyone would have risen in armed revolt.

Added to all that the water system worked haphazardly, if at all. The rooms with rickety bunk beds were extremely small and all night long you could hear the swish and trickle of water going along a large pipe at the end of your bed like a gang of drunk fairies rolling home after the office party. The metered heater had a mind of its own too; when mere money failed to get it going I found you could just pick it up and drop it on its head which sometimes did the trick. If it didn't, the only way to keep warm was actually to get into bed but the pillow was

so hard it might even have been modelled on St Columba's
original stone one.

The next morning we all gathered next to the stone cross of St
John for a pilgrimage around the island. A very strange gang of
pilgrims it was too: around 60 Germans in their Bavarian hats
and lederhosen, some greying elders of the Church of Scotland
in their walking boots and about 20 kids from Glasgow over for
a holiday in the abbey's community centre: dirty wee sparrows
with bruises all over their thin white legs, ill-fitting T-shirts
streaked with stains and thick brown coatings of nicotine on
their fingers. They had no leather bags or binoculars. They had
what they stood up in.

'This is not a race,' said our leader. 'It's walking together,
talking together and sharing the island together. This stone
cross has been here since 1200. Please shut all gates behind
you. Leave no litter. Only those over 75 can drop out.'

We made our way up a rubbled stone track, tiptoeing around
cow pats and across fields drowsy with daisies. Tiny hanks of
sheep's wool hung on the barbed wire fences. Even with flies
dive-bombing all around, everyone was cheerful and chattery as
the Glasgow kids each took it in turns to dump a fat girl on her
backside. But she always seemed able to bounce straight back
up, waving her beefy arms around and smiling in a way that
suggested she thought this was a lot of fun.

'Ah, zis is lousewourt,' said a German lady falling on her
knees and shoving her nose right up against a tiny blue flower.
'You see. It is insect-eating. Vunderbar.'

Later we squelched our way down a ravine that was half bog
and half rock until we came to an old marble quarry, its
machinery eaten away by rust since its closure in 1914. We
were asked to take a piece of marble and sing a hymn.

Boswell thought Iona was a fertile island; Sir Walter Scott
found it desolate and unbearable. But, just walking over these
dung-dotted slopes, you could see this small island of barely

three thousand acres was barely generous with itself. The tiny
reservoir was hardly enough for the island's population of 80 in
the winter – let alone in the summer when this number went
up fortyfold – and even then the brown water looked like
whisky. The soil was thin and sandy, whipped by centuries of
salt winds. Where there was no soil there was muddy bog with
small black slugs roving about and yellow irises so bitter not
even the starving sheep would eat them. For weeks during winter the wind blows with such destructive violence some abbey
workers move around with large rocks in their pockets to stop
themselves being blown over. Even the huge stone cross of St
John has been blown down twice.

But today the sun had got its hat on and we all streamed
over the golf course to St Columba's Bay. The waves were col-
lapsing and wheezing into the shingle; a group of brown cows
sat at one end of the beach like a small picnic party of fat,
horned day-trippers. It was here, in 563, that Columba and his
twelve disciples finally landed after a battle in Ireland where
3,000 had been killed. He came, he said, determined to convert as many to Christ as had died in that battle, and the cairn
next to the beach marked the spot where Columba's beloved
Ireland finally vanished from view. 'It became the cairn that
turned its back on Ireland,' said our guide. I picked up a shell
and listened to the anguished howling inside it.

A mini-van from the abbey came bumping across the field
and we all queued for our lunch: a plastic cup of tea from a
silver urn, a package of spam sandwiches and an apple. I have
always hated spam and apples but was so hungry I all but ate
the wrapping as well. We threw our apple stumps out for the
sheep.

I spent a happy half an hour talking with Tom, an East End
social worker who had come here with his wife for a break since
he had a serious chest complaint. He told me a bull had got
loose on the island the day before with everyone diving and
leaping over the hedgerows. Even poorly Tom had got over a
fence like he was Superman. 'The only time I want to see a bull
is inside a hamburger,' he added with a shiver.

Later we trooped across more fields and came to a ruined hermit's cell where the monks used to come to be silent with God. The guide asked us to be silent for three minutes and we sat around the rubble listening to the sounds as the monks would have heard them: to the skylark who seemed to have been busy whistling his brains out all day long; to the conversation between wave and shingle; to the thin beleaguered cries of the sheep and the wind quivering in the grass. To the medieval mind all such sounds had meaning.

By late afternoon many of the pilgrims had fallen away as we toiled up the final – and highest – hill on the island. There was a wonderful view of the sweep of the Inner Hebrides; of the rugged outline of Jura where Orwell wrote *Nineteen Eighty-Four*; of the innumerable caves of Staffa, including Fingal's Cave, immortalized by Mendelssohn; of the wild, torn slopes of Skye with her whisky stills . . . all dotted over the glittering blue waters like great grey battleships moving in for battle.

By now our faces were as pink as prawns from being out all day in the sun. We were quite tired too; not much chatter was left in us. Only the Glaswegian children were still leaping around as if they had just got up, though the fat girl, clearly fed up with her role as the group's ball, had gone missing. A few of us went off to a nearby well in which, according to pagan rite, if you washed your face, you could stay young forever, before tumbling down the iris-spattered slope and back to the abbey for a shower and snooze before dinner.

The night bells sounded in the glimmer din – as they charmingly call twilight here – and, dinner over, we crowded into the church for a healing service. Healing, in the traditions of Columba, is central to the abbey's work. There is a monthly intercession whereby people can write asking for prayers for someone. Lists of names are then sent to 130 intercessors scattered over the country and the sick are all then prayed for on a regular basis.

But tonight was to be a laying on of hands service. 'We see this as the very work of the church,' said the speaker. 'We do this because we have been commanded to do this. Mark said that believers will put their hands on the sick and they will be healed. Touch shows sympathy and empathy. It shows Christ's love and compassion for every person.'

A group of people filed up to the altar with the rest of the congregation coming up from behind, all placing their hands on one another and their sick brothers and sisters. *Lord, they whom thou lovest are sick.* It was a tender moment in the flickering half-light, some ministering to others in faith. It was somehow healing that so many Germans were with us too and, not for the first or last time on the island, I felt close to Columba, the great healer himself.

The weather was still acting as if it had taken a permanent lease on the sun when I got back to Oban but it was spitting with cold rain when, a day or so later, I got into St Andrews, a salt-blown, grey granite town of great age and no small loveliness. It overlooks a wild, wild sea with the ruins of a cathedral at one end and the famous golf course on the other, all built around the oldest university in Scotland. It soon emerged that there wasn't a bed to be had anywhere since I had arrived on a popular golfing weekend.

Indeed I only got a room at all by taking a family room and paying three times the single rate. This really annoyed me since it was clearly going to be empty had I not turned up and had I been a bit sharper I should have gone out and found two of the smelliest tramps in St Andrews to fill up the other two beds though I could not think that St Andrews had such things as smelly tramps. The place was clearly a snob of the first water and had abolished tramps long ago.

There is little more deadly and lacking in fun than the educated Scottish middle class and here, of course, we were in its very temple. The only cinema in St Andrews had long closed and the council had refused to let it be turned into a disco. The nearest disco was about five miles away but many stayed away from that because of the fights. The churches provided no social entertainment worth speaking of. The students also seemed extremely stuffy and kept themselves to themselves. All in all, growing up here must have been the most boring occupation imaginable. 'I'm an artist,' one youngster told me. 'I draw the dole.' Even worse than having nothing to do, they had nothing to say either.

That night I walked down near the cathedral where the steady splashing of waves mingled in the broken-jawed silhouettes. The rain clouds had cleared up by now; from somewhere in the town came the bright music of breaking glass. Patches of phosphorescent light broke up on the cobbles when a seagull came twirling around in the brightness, its long yellow beak screaming as if in pain before it flew away again. Stars glinted above when something moved and there was one of those beautiful, long, silent, enchanting slides of a shooting star falling through galaxy after galaxy.

Shooting stars always remind me of angelic activity; of some great angel going about its business from one end of the universe to another, possibly carrying some momentous news about developments in God's kingdom. If you want to know what an angel is like I will tell you. Your average angel is generally invisible, always unapproachable and does not suffer from human needs. They have their own distinct personalities, are mainly based in Israel but have each been assigned certain territories which they have been told to look after. They cannot be in more than one place at the same time and, contrary to popular belief, we only know of one with wings who can fly. An angel never ages or falls sick or feels randy. They do experience joy, particularly when a sinner repents. They do not marry, nor can they be given in marriage, though they do make an awful lot of music. They play harps continually and their language is Welsh.

As agents of God's will they are constantly active throughout the world, helping people, saving them from danger, delivering messages or even being instruments of revenge, sometimes carrying flaming swords. They are stronger than humans since it was they who rolled back the stone. In appearance, they might be swathed in radiant light, occasionally representing themselves in visions, burning bushes, dreams or even as humans.

Angels are capable of sin and it was because of Lucifer's sin of covetousness and pride that Michael booted him out of heaven after a momentous fight. It was then that Lucifer – the most beautiful son of the morning who had once walked proud on the holy mountain – came down among us where he has been causing nothing but trouble ever since.

The next morning I went back to explore the cathedral ruins properly. It is a total ruin, with just one high wall intact, yet the outline of the original church – built as the longest in Britain after Norwich – is easily discernible, the thin nave leading down to the twin turreted east gable. The west front archway is half missing, as though chopped down the middle by a giant cleaver. The grass lawns – at odds with the fragmented ruins and stone arches leading nowhere – are perfectly kept, the tombstones set out in regular marching lines. Just here was the worn head of a mitred churchman; over there the broken remains of a sanctuary wall.

There was a definite whiff of holiness here and no mistake. In spite of the ruin you can feel the strength of the old faith that built the place. Even in what is left you can see it was built with care as a beautiful argument for God and the assembly of his people.

The sky was gunmetal grey going on for stormy black when I arrived at Carfin, a scruffy, litter-blown mining village just outside Motherwell. It was almost as if the colour of the sky had seeped into the very council houses as they stood, back to concolorous back, in curving dejected lines as dogs sniffed around for interesting smells on the dandelion lawns. A milk van pulled up and a hooter sounded. A gang of kids came marauding down the pavement on mountain bikes, whizzing past the rubble and twisted iron of an old factory site. Just over the road was a mini-market run by Rashid and Bari – the windows heavily grilled – and way out in the distance the white and black pillars of smoke curled above the steelworks. Everything was so drab you wanted to run amok and paint a house a canary yellow or scatter crimson paint over the tired privet hedges or even grab one of those manky dogs and dye him a bright forget-me-not blue.

But not all is as it seems since smack in the middle of this industrial backwater – as unlikely and incongruous as a pork chop in a bar-mitzvah – is a huge and splendid grotto; a collection of glass chapel, shrine and statue, centred around a small lake and sprawling over some 20 acres of avenue, path, hedgerow and tree. There is a statue of St Francis atop a large knoll known as Mount Assisi and nearby a domed replica of the house in Nazareth. We were in the Lourdes of Scotland.

In a shed I found a collection of relics and the first thing I saw was a letter written in the hand of St Therese, 'The Little Flower', a French Carmelite nun and co-patroness of the grotto who had once seen a vision of the Virgin Mary. Next to the letter was one of the lilies she had worn on her head and a brick from the infirmary in which she had died. There was also an artificial rose which cured a child of heart disease; some charred bones from the Boxer uprising, together with yet more bones from St Gregory, St Osmund and other medieval saints; a carved wooden crucifix from an olive tree in the Garden of Gethsemane and some stones from Calvary and the Church of the Holy Sepulchre.

Later I had a chat with one of the grotto workers who took me to look at a heli-pad at the other end of the grotto. A heli-pad in a grotto? It seemed they had been given the word that the Pope had intended to visit Carfin the previous year by helicopter. A huge panic ensued since His Holiness would have nowhere to land so they duly moved a statue of St Andrew and built the thing. Sadly, as it turned out, the Pope had no intention of visiting Carfin so, with the bricks left over from the heli-pad, they built a bridge over the lake, which was another mistake since wheelchairs couldn't get over it.

A huge pilgrimage began that afternoon with pilgrims mostly coming in by chartered coach from such as Calderbank, Cumberland and Newcastle. There were grey old men with flat caps and folding chairs, women with bags from the Costa Brava, cub scouts with their faces as shining and scrubbed as little pickles, the wheelchair pilgrims and the young girls in their frothy white lace confirmation frocks, all as pretty and perfect as morning daisies. They brought with them a rising buzz of cheerful excitement as the green-sashed stewards directed them to their places around the lake. Way out over the fields, waving pillars of grey and white smoke belched out of the Ravenscraig steelworks. A burst of distorting static whined in the loudspeakers set up in the branches of the trees.

When the service had ended the pilgrims dispersed, some filling their bottles with holy water from the tap near the entrance or queuing to buy a souvenir from the grotto shop. It was only then I noticed the many women sitting around the benches, chortling merrily and producing vast piles of sandwiches and thermos flasks full of steaming tea which they distributed to the equally vast numbers of their families.

Many of them were beefy baby machines, disdainful of birth control and as durable as the plastic flowers and gilded polythene statues for which they seemed to have such a weakness. These were the very engines of the huge and inviolable families which were the peculiar if unfashionable triumphs of the Catholic faith. There was a whole procession of them, with great bosoms for the broken-hearted to sob on and broad backs to shoulder the greatest burdens. Some of their hands were as big as shovels, abrim with the maternal love that heals all hurts; that sustains through illness and poverty; that succours all, particularly the rejected and the handicapped; that takes the effort to turn out the little girls in such wonderful dresses; that, over the years, has peeled a good million tons of potatoes, washed a cathedral of windows and scrubbed a whole planet of floors.

These are the great sturdy oaks of motherhood, all come to give tribute to the most venerated mother of them all, Holy Mary, Mother of God.

## 4

# The Toughest Pilgrimage in the World

DOWNPATRICK · SAUL · BELFAST · DERRY ·
LOUGH DERG · KNOCK · WESTPORT

I began the Irish leg of my pilgrimage soaking up a beautiful,
balmy summer evening in the graveyard of Down Cathedral
in Downpatrick. Behind me a man, stripped to the waist, was
cutting a hedge with electric clippers. A dog barked and a
woman's voice shouted for it to keep quiet. I had heard a lot of
barking dogs around the town since I had arrived. Weeds and
nettles were springing up among the grey crosses and small
ashen statues on the tombstones. Vivid red puffs of poppies
were scattered around the graves, some but pods waiting to
burst and spread their seed. Graveyards are excellent places for
meditating on the cycles of life and death. Nettles in particular
thrive on the sulphates of human bones.

The sun slanted away behind me sending long thin shadows
stretching down the slopes. Gnats danced around my legs.
That dog barked again. Directly below me was a wooded valley
with the thin whine of passing traffic coming up out of it. Just
over on my right were the mountains of Mourne; one great
etching in purple, humped with great age and suffused with the
golden glow of the withdrawing sun. The song of a bird began
duelling with the barking of the dog. A leaf fell onto the grass
with the softest splash of noise. Then another. The mountains
were actually changing colour in the sunset, going from purple
to misty black and lightening in part to brown. The drifting
white smoke of three wood fires, soft white on hard black,

meandered the length of the mountains. A huge bird glided on the thermals overhead. The serenity of it all was quite magical: a perfect moment in a perfect creation just sitting there waiting for the great painter to come and capture all this sorrowing grandeur in oils. For the mountains were sorrowing – of that I had no doubt.

I had come to Downpatrick in Ulster by bus, first signing into Denvir's Hotel in English Street. The hotel is said to be more than three hundred years old and, to be fair, looked every second of it. There did not seem to be any other occupants either. In all the time I was there I only ever spoke to the affable lady who, with her sister, owned the place. She was hoping to sell it soon.

That afternoon I had gone to see Colin Crichton on the *Down Recorder*. He is a man of exquisite grooming and a silky voice who kept putting me in mind of the perfect creamy froth on the top of a pint of Guinness. He was also, it emerged, something of an amateur historian and archaeologist, telling me much about St Patrick and nearby Strangford Loch – 'the fastest tidal movement in Britain'. Patrick put up his first church in Ireland in neighbouring Saul.

With a population of 9,000, Downpatrick was overwhelmingly Catholic, he said. In spite of sectarian strife, both sides often came together to worship in the cathedral. Inevitably the conversation drifted to The Troubles; indeed, almost every conversation I had in Ulster drifted into the same wretched terminus. 'It's the media always talking of violence, it is,' said Colin. 'There's lovely, colourful things out here. Why don't you people from London come over and write about them?'

I couldn't agree more and said so. Yet it was not to talk about The Troubles that I had come to Downpatrick, but for the cathedral. Just over the other side of the graveyard was the burial place of Patrick, marked with a Celtic cross and a large grey stone slab in the shadow of a yew tree. The name PADRAIG was discernible amidst the pinky white patches of lichen. Columba and Bridget were also said to be buried in this grave.

'In Down three saints one grave fill, Brigid, Patrick and Columcille.'

Still glorying in the voluptuous twilight I walked around the graveyard and into the cathedral. The sun was sending long golden bars across the nave. I was immediately confronted by the organ erected on the choir screen. It sits in a huge Gothic case and is an instrument so perfect and so complete and so original, it says in the guidebook, it is the most broadcast in Ireland.

There was no one around when I walked down the aisle – and no sounds either, just the sad pungent smell of damp. Much of the plasterwork was clearly spalling and falling away with enough damp seeping through those walls to give a dozen snails rheumatism. They say it will take a quarter of a million pounds to fix it.

A beautiful gold cross sat on the altar beneath a stained glass work featuring many of the saints. The pews were brown and polished, with a rude granite christening font and a bishop's throne set in the middle of the congregation. This, again according to the guidebook, symbolizes the Shepherd with his flock around him. Most interesting of all were the cornices on top of the pillars, all of them different. One showed the tonsured head of a cleric with, on each side, two villains attacking him with ravenous, evil jaws. No change there, then.

The ubiquitous John Wesley came here in 1778 when the cathedral was a ruin. He wrote in his journal:

> At the head of English Street stands the Abbey on the hill. It is a noble ruin, the largest building I have seen in the kingdom. Adjoining it is one of the most beautiful groves covering the side of a sloping hill.

Wesley preached in that grove though there were, of course, few places he had not spoken in. Travelling a hundred miles a week, 5,000 miles a year, his Call took him the equivalent of nine times around the world. He preached 40,000 sermons.

When I asked a lady at the cathedral door to show me the

grove where Wesley spoke, she pointed down through some trees. These days, she said, the police went down there every night. It was where the local teenagers gathered to put drugs up their noses.

The sun dipped over the mountains but there was still plenty of light in the sky. I followed a wooded lane down to a meadow where there was a lovely, still lake which erupted in a flapping explosion of ducks and moorhens when I walked up to the bank. It might have been on this very bank that Patrick knelt with a prayer of thanks after he had been returned to Ireland.

It might also have been an unreal radiance like this which spread over the land for the twelve days after his burial when there was no darkness at all and hymns and canticles were sung for his soul throughout Ireland.

I went over to his original church in Saul the next day and found a powerful wee church built out of light-grey Mourne granite. Its design, with its pointy, pencil-shaped tower, is based on the early Christian church. Inside there are some stones thought to come from Patrick's original abbey, though all that remains of the abbey today is one powdering wall with ivy lapping around it and two small corbelled cells, which may have been used by anchorites but are now overgrown by every weed that ever enjoyed a picnic in a graveyard.

I met an old man in the nave and asked him how many people came along to worship here these days.

'Let me see now. On the last count there was 24 families and, the way it's going, soon there'll be no more.'

'You've been getting no converts then?'

'None. When we die the church dies.'

'God not doing too well around here then?'

'Not in this country he's not.'

Something dark and fleeting darted in his eyes like a fish diving deep for cover and he turned away to cough into his hand. I recognized the dart in those eyes. It was the sudden realization that an old and faithful Christian had lost his faith too; that he shouldn't really have said that but now it was said anyway.

So the cycle of belief and unbelief had swung its full course. Even in this very church, where Patrick had first brought the good news to the Irish, there were those who had been sustained and nourished by that news all their lives but who had now lost it; those who had cast out certainty for doubt; those who believed that all those hours of worship had been in vain.

It was only that momentary look in the old man's eyes that made me realize the awesome extent of The Troubles in Ulster; that, in this country, the fear and hatred had become so pervasive that they had not only destroyed families and homes but had attacked the very mind and thought of God too.

Holiness had been swept out of Ulster. Holiness had died since the demons, which Patrick had fought with such energy and faith, had returned to the land. The spirit of the Druids was again abroad in the streets and fields. Oh, to be sure, they had come back in a different form and by different means but they were alive and well on every hearth in this long and terrifying season of black rain.

There was little doubt in my mind about the nature of these modern demons who masqueraded under the banners of the satellite dish and the television aerial. These demons are technological and the children of corrupt thought. These demons come in flashing, elusive images and are pulling this society apart just as surely as the Druidic demons of old. The very fabric of Christian love has been eaten away by these demons who have divided the community into armed and hating camps. They are the demons who nest in the cave of the media, persistently seizing on the wicked and odious imagery of the knee-cappings, the tar and featherings, the riots, the burned-out houses, the shattered glass, the explosions . . . then transforming them into bustling, savage agents of hatred – the same evil children of the Druids who were once routed by Patrick's Paschal fire on the hill of Slane. They are all back with us in force and more destructive than ever.

It is not the terrorist events as such which are important or significant. It is the mind which gathers them all up and then pours them down onto every hearth. It is this violence-loving mind of the modern media which is the mother and father of these new Ulster demons, and if this mind, which feeds and rewards violence with global publicity and significance, was removed from the community, this strife would be over within a year. Love would be restored and stability returned. The spirit of St Patrick, who loved everyone equally regardless of their faith, would reach across the divides again and heal the wounds.

Or so God once explained to me in a series of visions.

The most surprising feature of Belfast is the magnificence of its setting. It is ringed by high hills and sits on a misty lough overhung by the giant crucifix cranes of the Harland and Wolff shipyard. The suburbs could be the suburbs of any European city but, as you travel towards the city centre, certain things begin to lodge in your mind; the wire grilles, the swathes of barbed wire, the mirrors to see around corners and the closed circuit television cameras. There are also lots of empty houses with the windows blocked up by breeze blocks.

I have been here many times – too many times really – largely as a reporter with some posh Sunday paper or other, but I still find the city deeply shocking and am never prepared for it – the rubbled sites, the sooty whorls left by the petrol bomb, the armed policemen in flak jackets and the routine Army patrols. This was a city at war but you couldn't quite work out who with. This was a city where something had gone deeply wrong but you couldn't quite be sure how or where.

I took a room in a guest house near the university and went over to the Botanic Gardens, looking around the tropical plants in the Palm House then lying down on the grass in the sunshine. A shadow flitted over the yellow blaze in my closed eyes followed by a thump on the grass next to me. David.

He was a wee scruff of a boy in a T-shirt on which was written: 'Here Comes Trouble'. We got chatting; rather he did all the chatting, giving me a lot of information about himself and occasionally allowing me to say yes or no, nothing more.

He was seven. His Ma was going to get him new shoes the next day. His Da had gone to heaven. His Ma was sitting on the bench over there. Would I like to go and meet her? Could he jump over me again? Be my guest.

He jumped over me a few more times then his non-stop chatter returned. Did I have a big knife at home? Did I have a big knife to stick into someone if he upset me? He wanted a big knife when he grew up. He would like to get a real gun too. Would I like to meet his Ma? Best of all he was good at throwing things. Those flowers over there. Could he go and pull them up? Come over and meet his Ma.

After a while his Ma came over and apologised for him, scooping him under her arm and taking him away. I lay back on the grass thinking about the child's words, his anxieties and insecurities, his fascination with big knives and destroying things. For surely this was the way a whole generation of young minds had been slaughtered here in Ulster. Yes, that was the way of it all right.

I walked out of the gardens and cars roared past as I stood next to a lamp-post, marooned in a city afternoon, with a few old newspapers rolling around the gutter near my feet. Yes, we all had children in Belfast. There was a part of us all in this city in this season of black rain.

The next day I took off for Derry, finding the city sitting next to a fat, curling river with sunshine burnishing her rooftops and a swarm of starlings bundling around the chimney pots. But again you began picking up certain discords as you moved through her streets: the Republican flags flying over the flatlands of the Bogside and the Union Jacks fluttering in other areas; the burned-out and bricked-up buildings, yet more miserable monuments to this appalling sectarian strife which must hurt God so much.

Here, if anything, the devastation was more complete than in Belfast. It struck you wherever you looked. I was mooching about in the graveyard of St Columba's Cathedral, way up on a hill inside the old walled city, when I bumped into a police-man, his fierce black eyes regarding me with suspicion. He held a rifle at the ready; you somehow don't expect to bump into armed men in graveyards. I didn't say anything and withdrew in some confusion. It was only later I learned the cathedral is next to the courthouse and, that day, there was a terrorist in the dock.

I decided to walk around the old wall ramparts, barely a mile long and a pleasant enough hobble but I might have been walk-ing through a nightmare what with the broken glass and con-crete bunkers. Everywhere, on every spare bit of wall, there were coloured swathes of graffiti, those flowery epitaphs we always find in dying cities. PROVOS OK. STUFF THE FENI-ANS. UP THE BRITISH ARMY. Every hundred yards or so there were giant concrete bunkers smothered with rolls of barbed wire and telescopes with which the Army could keep an eye on any unruly elements in the Bogside. Through a slit I saw a visored face watching me looking at him. Even as I lifted my hand and made a little wave of friendliness I could see the butt of his rifle moving along the slit, ready no doubt in case my friendly gesture turned into a swinging hand about to hurl a petrol bomb.

But it was while looking around the cathedral again that I bumped into the verger, Bobby Jackson, a man of the purest enchantment who, as soon as I looked at him, told me my visit to this beleaguered city had not been in vain.

He had a tiny shrunken head mounted on a long neck with big, floppy ears, bushy eyebrows and the tightest, smallest mouth. He said he was 'just 83' and the oddness of his appear-ance was made considerably odder by the fact that he was as bald as a snooker ball with tiny red veins running about his boko like a relief map of the rivers of the world. The whole of his amazing head positively glistened as if it had been given a tremendous once-over with floor polish.

When I met him in the vestry he was shining a communion cup and singing to himself: 'Oh to be sure I'm the happiest man that ever walked on two legs.' And what was the reason for all this happiness? Well, he'd been having the very divil of trouble with the graveyard gates but now workmen were out there fixing them and making him happier than ever.

He showed me around the various war mementoes in the museum, together with the bomb mounted on a small plinth in the porch. This bomb was fired into Derry by an invading Irish army in 1689. It did not explode and instead was found to contain a letter offering the most favourable terms to the besieged loyalists if they would surrender the city. They had been besieged for 85 days and a lot of them had died, the survivors living chiefly on starch mixed with tallow. Nonetheless they still refused to give in.

All his life, Bobby said, he had got up at 5 a.m. and worked through to 6 p.m. for just half a crown a week. No tea-break. Nothing. But look what the workers got these days. 'I was watching this man painting, so I was, and he was painting over some dog mess he was. I said you should clean that, I said. No pride, that's the trouble these days. My belief is that plenty of hard work keeps you young. That's my experience too. I raised a big family. I had no broo or assistance. I had to go out for money to feed them. We got nothing from the British Government but now they take seven pounds twenty tax a week off me from what I earn here.' It was then he told me he had no less than 24 children.

Later that morning there was a tiny communion service with a congregation of ten in the small chapel on one side of the nave. Afterwards I had a long chat with the Dean, the Very Reverend George Good. I asked him if Bobby really had 24 children. 'He does,' was the reply. 'Twenty-four children and a very tired wife.'

Bobby specialized in the year 1689 and knew everything about it, the Dean said. Even today, he maintained the tradition of ringing the curfew bells at 9 a.m. and 9 p.m. It wasn't true he was always happy; if he was wearing a cap that meant trouble. People suspected he was even older than he said. 'The locals say he's really 88 and that he decided to leave out the war years.'

It turned out that Bobby had come to them one day to act as a relief verger and the first indication that he had become permanent came when he painted his name on the bottom of the church notice-board. Bobby had lost his hair through shock when he had been upended into the brass funnel of a fire engine during a riot on the Bogside. All his hair fell out the same night. The astonishing sheen of his head always posed problems when the television cameras were in the cathedral. The technicians kept on powdering his head since his boko kept catching the lights and glowing like a great belisha beacon.

The Dean was an affable man with an engaging sense of humour but with the strange and disconcerting habit when talking of making his eyeballs disappear as his eyelashes fluttered up and down to show a vast expanse of white. He had been here 16 years – just one and a half before the balloon went up – and they were doing what they could to keep the spirit of Columba alive in the wreckage.

'I know all the members of the other churches by their Christian names. We meet a lot and the Catholic clergy come to services here. The Presbyterians won't mix with the Catholics though.'

He added that they tried hard to keep the notion of pilgrimage alive; indeed, a few years back, to commemorate the fourteen hundred years since Columba sailed from Londonderry, the cathedral had arranged for 13 people to row a curragh following Columba's original voyage. 'When they arrived in Iona the mist was so thick a bishop got lost in it.'

They still celebrated Columba's birthday every year but it had to be remembered that this was not the site of the original church. He unlocked a large vault and pulled out some old and probably valuable maps, showing the Church of the Long Tower, just a mile or so from the cathedral. This was Columba's original church.

Later I walked down into the Catholic enclave to have a look at the Church of the Long Tower, yet another oasis in the general devastation of grilles and yet more burned-out houses. Inside three people were praying amidst lots of polished wood and banks of glimmering devotional candles. It was here that Columba said his first Mass in Derry in 546, according to a stone.

I stood staring at the steady and bright flames of the candles. Such flames tell us much about what is holy. They tell us about the unbroken flow of prayer which continues even after our private prayers have stopped. They tell of the light that Christ brings into our lives. They symbolize the spiritual daring of Patrick's Paschal flame when he defied the evil demons of the Druids.

I took a candle and lit one for that boy in the Botanic Gardens in Belfast. I took another and lit it for embattled Ulster with a quiet prayer that a great ball of purifying fire might be rolled across the Province and free it from the destructive influence of this new man of lawlessness. I lit another in the prayer that the loving spirit of Columba would return to this city and this church where it was first given majestic birth. I lit another with Elijah in mind who, after long years of prayer and hope, saw the first clouds of rain on the horizon after a long, long drought. Jesus said: 'I am the light of the world.'

There were about a hundred of us standing on the quay, all as quiet and thoughtful as communicants queuing up at the altar rail for the bread and wine. It was the greyest of mornings – a moisty morning, as the Irish say – with the glittering still waters in front of us and the wooded low hills of Donegal behind. Far out on the lake a grey building with a green dome rose sheer out of one of the many islands and sat on the water like a magical illusion. It might have been a French chateau or even a Victorian prison but it was the Basilica of St Patrick's Purgatory of Lough Derg.

We were all quiet and thoughtful since each of us had just paid six pounds in the ticket office and were about to spend three days and two nights in the toughest and most penitential pilgrimage in the world.

As requested, none of us had eaten since the night before and already the hunger pains were gnawing my belly. I was with Felix, a small, bald man, as old as those hills and with the lithe fitness of a flea. On the bus down here he had been teaching me how to say the Rosary and its prayers which, for the next three days, we would be reciting endlessly. *Hail Mary full of grace for the Lord is with ye. Blessed art thou amongst women and blessed is the fruit of thy womb Jesus Christ.* Now you say it yourself, said Felix. Right. Now the Creed: *I believe in God, the Father Almighty, the maker of heaven and earth.* Now the Our Father. *Our Father which art in heaven hallowed be thy name...*

Felix had been to Lough Derg more times than he could remember. One year he had come with a bad back; it had healed up on the penances. 'You never take a cold home from Lough Derg,' he told me, but I knew that more than one pilgrim had died from the island's rigours. Then again, one man had made a grand total of 56 visits, the last when he was well into his eighties.

The sky was blackening and curdling with thunder as our boat chugged across the water, sending out bobbing waves which whooshed along the banks of the tiny islands choked with shrubs and small ash trees. The water was a rusty colour – hence Lough Derg, the Red Lake. A peal of bells rang out and soon we were disembarking into one of the strangest encounters I have had with a place anywhere.

More than a thousand people were crammed together on this small island, some sitting on benches and others walking around the untidy brown stones which formed the penitential beds. All were barefoot and watched us silently as we came ashore and walked up past the dank lawns. It was their silence which was so difficult to come to terms with.

I followed Felix up to a dormitory where a nun, dressed in grey robes and with wide severe features that seemed not to have been creased by too much laughter, told us to take off our shoes and socks and leave all our belongings on one of the beds. I pressed my fingers into the mattress, finding no give at all. 'They *are* hard,' said the nun, watching me. 'But when you do come to sleep here you won't even notice it.'

And so, barefoot and holding a rosary, I came out into the warm, damp yard where a fresh-faced priest with spiky ginger hair explained what I had to do. 'First you have to make a station. You start here at St Patrick's Cross where you kneel and say one Our Father, one Hail Mary and one Creed. Then you go to St Bridget's Cross . . .'

One whole station, I discovered, called for an hour of kneeling before and kissing crosses, circling the Basilica again and again, walking repeatedly around the stone beds of St Brendan, St Catherine and St Columba, kneeling on the shore facing the lake and pushing out your arms three times at St Bridget's Cross to renounce the world, the flesh and the devil. All prayers were to be said standing, walking or kneeling – but never sitting.

In between each station you could rest but you had to accomplish at least three stations before the beginning of the all-night vigil in the Basilica.

I began my first station sticking right behind Felix but he soon left me behind and I fell into a strange, uplifting, wearying pattern of prayer and discomfort circling around and around with the others. Bells rang out occasionally; now and then my feet slipped or I stubbed my toes on the rocks of the penitential beds which were the remaining ruins of the beehive cells of the first Celtic anchorites who once lived here. Their dampness made them difficult to walk on and even worse to kneel on. I doubted if I was going to survive three days of this; in fact, at the start, I wouldn't have put money on me lasting three hours.

But I did settle down and after two stations was relaxed enough to begin nosing around to see what was going on. My most vivid and immediate impression of the place was the horrific ugliness of human feet. There were swollen feet with bulging blue veins and hammered toes. There were puffed-up ankles and feet with bunions and corns. All of them were stinking dirty from walking through the mud of the penitential beds though even the thickest layers of mud could not disguise those awful patterns – some flat and others fallen, some twisted and others skeletal, some knobbly and others bunched with arthritis. We spent a lot of time obsessing about feet on Lough Derg.

Yet in between stations we discussed lots of other things too since the Irish clearly can't give up yarning, not even on a penitential pilgrimage. By and large they were a jolly, devout bunch with hunched shoulders and grey hair. But there was a fair smattering of teenagers too, all eager to do their stations properly and not above telling the odd dirty joke to show how worldly they really were. 'So this priest asked me if I had ever slept with a woman and I said, oh to be sure, I must have dozed off a couple of times.'

They were dressed in a variety of jogging suits, football jerseys and jeans. They smoked a lot between their stations too, which I thought a bit unfair on us non-smokers since the cigarettes took the edge off their hunger. Mine was now positively burning the pit of my belly. Later that afternoon we went for our first and only meal of the day: not steak and chips exactly but dry toast and black tea, perched on a long bench next to a trestle table. As a meal it did bank down the worst excesses of our hunger and most took it in good humour. There were also some flinty oatmeal cakes, so dry and unappetizing they were largely left untouched.

No one bends the rules on food or rest, as I discovered from one of the priests, who told me of two women who came here and produced their own bottle of milk for their tea. The priest pointed out this was not allowed and the women insisted they had been given a special dispensation by the Archbishop of Dublin. A brisk row followed when the Prior, Gerard McSorley, was called and the next thing the two women, together with their bottle of milk, were on the boat back to the mainland.

Other pilgrims have been sent home for turning up drunk or, in one case, for bringing a rug to snuggle down under at night. An unbelievable amount of thought and effort had gone into making you as uncomfortable as possible. You are locked out of your dormitory. There is no pulling leg warmers down over your feet; without shoes or socks feet get cold and stay cold. Sweets, chocolate and chewing gum are banned. Apart from the tea, the only thing you may drink is Lough Derg soup: warm water which may be sprinkled with salt or pepper or even *both*. Mineral water is allowed which, for the purposes of the fast, is defined as anything which does not fizz – i.e. water out of a tap.

Evening Mass was in the Basilica at 6.30. The Reverend Michael Hand spoke of love: 'Too many people are confused by what we mean by love. There are confused ideas particularly among the young. So what do we mean by love? Is it a feeling or an emotion? Jesus' whole life is a living description of love. The essence of Christianity is to love to the point of death. Paul's is a perfect portrait of love. "Love is always patient and kind . . . never rude or selfish. Delights in the truth." How do we measure up to this idea of love? We must love people as they are. It is easy to love those who love us. But our love may meet with hatred and rejection sometimes. We must not be afraid to stand up and be counted. Jesus won in the end. He loved unto death.'

For that service there were 1600 of us packed into the three galleries of the Basilica – the largest number of pilgrims to come to Lough Derg in one day and 233 more than the number who came on the same day the previous year. Back in the 1950s 33,000 came in one season but numbers declined in the 1960s and 1970s. Just 20,000 came in 1982. But, this season, it looked as if they were going to have the largest number ever, since, as one priest believed, times of poverty and hardship were again encouraging people to return to the Lord.

Without curtains or flowers the lantern-shaped Basilica reflected the austerity which is the pure spirit of this particular penance. The nave was set before a plain white marble altar; a giant chandelier hung down from the roof like clusters of bright electric berries. The plain walls rose in clear straight lines though it was the stained glass windows which provided the one touch of colour, depicting the Stations of the Cross in terrific daubs of yellows, reds and purples.

Announcements followed the sermon: 'If you haven't taken your meal for the day you should do so as soon as possible. There will be confessions at 8.30 for those who have completed three stations.'

After the service our little gang met again on the bench near the water's edge where we shared yarns, jokes and the odd bit of helpful advice. 'When you go for confession go for the Pilgrim Priest cubicle,' said Danny. 'He's a Franciscan and will absolve you from everything you've ever done. You don't even have to say much. They're flying out of that cubicle like bullets. Franciscans only get upset by sins against charity.'

Asking about, I found a great variety of motives for coming on this pilgrimage. Some had come to pray for work, to seek a favour in examinations or to try to make a decision on whether to get engaged or even to leave home. Some had come in a spirit of thanksgiving for some Divine favour. One man had promised, 40 years ago, that he would do this pilgrimage if his sister recovered from a serious illness. She had indeed recovered and so – a little late in the day, to be sure – here he was. Those who came out of curiosity never came back; curiosity was soon satisfied here.

Come 9.30 p.m. and it was time for the night prayer and benediction. Two bats were yawing around inside the Basilica dome and there was a slight burble of conversation as we packed into the pews. Then we sang a hymn as, outside, the night thickened over the placid yeasty waters of the lake and the midges danced around inside the lights of the yard. A boat came in, sending its wake chuckling up against the quay. Some would soon be going to bed but we, who had arrived that day, were getting ready for the Rite of Penance which would take us through a night of tributes to St Patrick for rescuing us from the devastation of sin.

'Your beds must have been locked up and you must remember that you must not lie down anywhere or stretch yourself out.

You must not get down on your front or your back or prop yourself up on your elbow. If you do we will ask you to sit up. When
I do they always say: "But father, I wasn't sleeping." Stay off the
grass. Let the grass look after itself. You must always sit with
your back against something. Some even fall asleep standing
up. But remember the pilgrimage is not invalid if you do nod
off. It only becomes invalid when you cease to make a decent
effort. All these things you are doing are to bring you closer to
God. Remember also that even before the world was created
God knew you would be here tonight. This brings us to the
mystery of human freedom and God's plan to bring us together.

'Lough Derg teaches us the value of prayer; the value of
being tough on ourselves; making time for God; being prepared to be a Christian in public. Faith must be the foundation
stone on which all else is built. So keep your mind on the Lord
and don't just sit there gazing at the bunion on the foot of the
person in front of you.'

And so, with the ritual closing of the Basilica doors to symbolize those fearful hours when St Patrick battled with demons
in a cave on this very island, the Rite of Penance began. A man
ascended the pulpit and began reciting the Hail Mary into a
microphone. We joined in. *Hail Mary full of grace for the Lord
is with ye*, he intoned, the words quickening and merging in a
sort of long, electrified buzz. *Blessed art thou amongst women and
blessed is the fruit of thy womb Jesus Christ. Holy Mary Mother of
God pray for us sinners now and at the hour of our death.*

The congregation kept moving around and around inside
and outside the Basilica as we went through the Hail Marys, the
Our Fathers and Creeds. *Our Father which art in heaven hallowed be thy name . . . On the third day he rose again. He ascended
into heaven . . . I believe in the Holy Spirit . . .*

Throughout that penal night we were to chant aloud an
incredible 396 Our Fathers, 124 Creeds and 648 Hail Marys.

There is a strange Jesuitical cunning in the endless repetition
of these prayers since it is almost impossible to let your mind

stray from the words and their meanings as they echo through your consciousness. Any fantasies that begin forming are swiftly cut down. Pretend prayer is impossible. It is the method of the mantra in which meaning builds up in layers. The words might mean nothing, then they might mean everything. One minute they might be the empty cry of parrots and the next they are the profoundest insights of the greatest prophets. They might drift to you from a distance before erupting out of the very core of your being, be as soothing as a lullaby or as painful and direct as a knife in your side.

And so we chanted on throughout the long, shuffling, stumbling night.

Around four o'clock the words began losing their edge. Often they became gabbled, run together so they sounded like the gibberish of a lunatic. When kneeling someone next to you might sway and knock into you. It was so hard on the knees; one man took off his cap, put it down on the floor, went to kneel on it and then stopped, as if unsure if he could get his knees directly on it. So he went down on one knee and rearranged the position of his cap. Immediately it was time to get up and begin walking again. *Hail Mary full of grace the Lord is with ye . . .*

At the end of each station we got off this constantly revolving, kneeling world for some fifteen minutes' rest. Line after line of us in the pews were nodding off like drugged budgerigars; one man was even snoring until a sharp jab in the ribs woke him up again. Others went out for a smoke in the shelter outside; with all the fug and the packed, tired bodies it was starting to look like the waiting room of a Bombay railway station.

One woman passed around a canister to spray our feet; the midges had been attacking our bunions and corns. Some of the old stagers treated their feet with methylated spirits, always seeming to take things so easily, with their large smiles and little jokes for everything.

Five o'clock came and, walking around and around the outside of the Basilica, I wondered if it could possibly get any worse. It promptly started to pour with cold rain but still we kept trudging on . . . *I believe in the Holy Catholic Church, the communion of saints and* . . .

With the rain came a dawn as dark as a hangman's stare. Clouds of tiny moths had been hatched in the glooming light which was spreading out over the mirrored lake and the tiny granite fists of the islands in a great dripping symphony of twisting greys and mordant blacks. The whole universe seemed to be spreading up and outwards like a growing bubble and it was then that I believed I glimpsed something deep and rich in the Irish psyche.

This was not the bomb-throwing Irish so beloved of the media but a nation in her purest and most noble posture. This was the seed-bed of the Celtic Church; the great spiritual energy of a fundamentally decent people still prepared to stumble red-eyed through the night; still prepared to punish their knees in prayer before a holy God; still prepared to suffer the pangs of an outrageous hunger; still prepared to walk barefoot over hard stones as they chanted their tiny litanies of love . . . all so that they could earn the right to drag themselves face to face with their beloved Patrick; that they might look up to the monumental majesty of their saint who suffered so much when he bargained with God to ensure the faith and future of the Irish; the man who fought demons for them. For them!

This damp dawn we were all there in a fellowship of suffering with Patrick. His ineluctable personality was there with us, next to us, below us and above us. We were now suffering as he had once for us. We had come to pay homage to him; this complete man who comforted us still.

So, with the night behind us, the rain stopped and we stumbled on into the day, somehow not so tired now that the night hours were no longer calling us to our beds, just moving around our stations in slow amiable trances and still gathering down on the quay in between stations for a wee crack.

A few of us were sitting there with our aching feet dangling in the water when the cruellest thing happened. Someone in the priory was cooking bacon and egg whose smell drifted over the water towards us, churning over our empty bellies and almost lifting us up on tip-toe with the mesmerizing deliciousness of its aroma. There were a few wry smiles but nothing was said. There was nothing to say.

I did go up to the dormitory later that morning to clean my teeth. Taking one look at my bed I climbed on it and was fast asleep within seconds. But the nun with mirthless features caught me and threw me out. I hurried out without complaint or comment since I found her as terrifying as a London taxi driver.

But I sinned again soon after that. I found a can of Coca-Cola in my bag so I sat in the lavatory, my underpants wrapped around the tin to keep down the noise of its fizzing, and drank it with grateful relish.

Then we were back for the last few hours on those penitential beds. Sluggish minutes crawled past on torpid feet. Some of the beds were ankle deep in mud from the rain; I simply could not have felt any worse and consoled myself with the thought that, in olden days, the pilgrimage here lasted for nine days with just bread and water. Some pilgrims died of typhoid; everyone had to plunge themselves into the lake three times each day as a symbol of cleansing. Pilgrims were also armed with long pins which they stuck into anyone who dozed off in the night vigil.

And so it did finally come to 10 p.m., time for the night prayer, benediction and bed. We stumbled to our dormitories and, without a word and without even taking off our clothes, climbed on our rock-hard beds and it was Goodnight Vienna. No sooner had my eyes closed than it was time to get up again. It was the deepest, most complete and refreshing sleep I have ever had.

After morning prayer it was a joy to get our shoes and socks on again. To the call of a bugle, we all filed down to the boats and Father McSorley sang us the traditional hymn of farewell as we moved off.

It had been a remarkable visit; a bit like moving on a time warp back into the fifth century. Even as I looked around at the brown and grey hills and the ruins of deserted houses I was still not sure what had hit me. I had not done battle with demons but even a few weeks later I still felt a deep and mysterious sense of renewal. It was an encouraging feeling and there and then, on that boat, I promised I would do Lough Derg again but better. No slipping into bed, no mineral water that fizzes or any heretical stuff like that.

Knock turned out to be a tiny and bewildering village built around a main street in a low spin of green Mayo hills which, on first blush, had all the convivial vulgarity of a long and amplified belch. A sign in the middle of the place managed to sum it all up. *Confessions*, one way. *Holy Water*, the other. *Post Office*, this way. *Tourist Office*, that way. *Holiday Home*, up there. *Jeweller*, down there. *Assembly Rooms*, over the road.

The place could well have been the ugly offspring of a mating between a circus big top and a holiday camp, all crushed up into a hamburger with lots of chips and a single votive candle flickering on top of the lot. There were the great grey vistas of the car parks and the huge space-age church which not so much resembled a church as a rocket launching pad. Tiny rows of souvenir stalls stood next to the restaurants. There were admin offices for this and admin offices for that, and fast-food restaurants with even faster prices catering, miserably, for the hungry pilgrims.

The truly fatal feature of Knock – fatal because it is the first thing you notice on arrival – is the glittering torrent of plastic rubbish piled up over the counters like some beast hatched in the very maw of Woolworth's, growing and multiplying like that monster in *The Blob*, soon to devour the very church itself with the jaws of its kitsch crassness. On one stall alone I found plastic crucifixes, magnetic car badges, polythene bottles of Holy Water and pink shillelaghs of rock with *A present from Knock* written through them. There were also Knock baseball caps, holy bottle openers, polythene Celtic crosses and six-feet long wooden rosaries.

One small old church was amok with a wedding that afternoon. The lovely bride was standing in the porch with a smile on her lips frozen with the purest fear. Every now and then she tried to broaden the smile, but it was as if the corners of her mouth had been set in cement. The smile stretched a shade, collapsed and died. Crowds seemed to be drifting in and out of the nave with other pilgrims walking around and around the church fingering rosaries and chanting their Hail Marys. Before the wedding service began, a beautiful Irish tenor voice up in the gallery sang John Denver's 'Annie's Song'.

'We have come here to marry Thomas and Mary who have loved one another for a long time,' said the priest. 'We ask Our Lady to keep their love faithful and undying. The Christian home makes Christ present in all things. Love is his constant calling – his fulfilment and help.'

After the wedding vows people went up to the altar for communion. It occurred to me then how important a role the Church still plays in almost all life events – of how she is always there and active in matters of births, marriages and deaths. Even at a time when many see the Church as stumbling and failing she is still the very cement of society, interpreting and declaring God's eternal purpose, overseeing life's cycles of feast and fast, Sunday and weekend, Christmas and Easter, the sowing and the harvest.

We need to go back over a hundred years, to a rainy August 21, 1879, to understand how this huge shrine at Knock came into being.

These were famine-haunted years with the potato crop failing repeatedly and the farmers plagued by evictions by the army, rack rents and typhus. In 30 years the country had lost one third of its population – a million dead by famine and two

million in despairing flight. Now the crop was about to fail
again.

At 7 p.m. on that fateful August day the Mayo sky was slate
grey with a strong northerly wind blowing when Margaret
Beirne locked up the church in Knock for the night and set off
home. There was a fine drizzle when she noticed an orb of light
on the gable end of the church but, the evening being wet, she
continued home. Later at 7.30 p.m. she decided to take another
look and saw what looked like some white statues. Then, with
a friend, she saw that the statues were moving. 'It's the Blessed
Virgin,' said Margaret. Others were called and soon fifteen vil-
lagers were standing in the rain gazing at this apparition.

Three figures were moving slowly around an altar. Each figure
glowed with a startling and pure light. The flashing wings of
hovering angels were also in evidence. The central figure was
Mary dressed in a brilliant white cloak fastened at the neck with
a crown on her head. A beautiful mystical rose was attached to
her brow. Her hands were raised as if in prayer and her eyes
turned upwards to the drizzling skies. Her face, said one witness,
was a slightly yellower white than her cloak.

On her right was St Joseph and on her left St John the Evangelist holding an open book in his left hand and wearing the
robes of a bishop and 'a little roundy hat'. Behind St John was
an altar and, completing this fantastic arrangement of ice and
flame, a cross and a lamb.

This was clearly their beloved Mary, the Queen of Heaven,
come with a mother's faithful love, to tell her hungry children
they had not been forgotten as they struggled through their
own long, dark night.

People were flinging handfuls of confetti over the bride and
groom. The bride was indeed very lovely, more relaxed now it
was all over, with a broad grin lighting up her face. The groom
could not stop beaming either, his nose curled up and carna-
tioned chest puffed out like an extremely happy parrot.

On the gable end of this church there is now a glass oratory in which the three figures of the original apparition have been recreated in white Carrera marble. The glass door of the oratory had been slid back and pilgrims were now queuing up to kneel before the statuary. PLEASE DO NOT TOUCH THE STATUARY, read the inevitable notice.

But I continued to feel very uneasy in the place. Looking around the oratory, I found a golden rose which had been presented to the shrine by Pope John Paul. The rose was somehow in the character of the place. I recalled a poetry contest in Spain where the third prize was a gold rose, the second prize was a silver rose and the first prize was a real rose.

Right in the middle of the complex was a huge stone cross erected in memory of the Papal visit on September 30, 1979. 'The greatest event in Irish history since the coming of St Patrick.'

Later, I went to have a look at the huge new Basilica which had been built a few hundred yards away. With the space and functionalism of an aeroplane hangar, its interior echoed with the cries of distant children. Though full of light there was very little colour, whatever there once might have been seemed to have seeped away into the concrete support pillars. The chairs were small, cheap and wooden. There was no stained glass and no way of kneeling. Up above was a control room for radio and television while the altar sat in the middle of it all, cold and unadorned – a funeral pyre in the centre of a circus big top waiting patiently for a client.

Night was now spreading over Knock with a light mackerel sky and a long bank of fluffy black cloud moving over the distant horizon. In the main street a man was speaking so loudly in an illuminated *Telefon* kiosk his voice carried clear across the road. A huge flock of starlings were roosting on a tall television mast – bundles of fat musical notes dotted over the lines of the wires.

I walked back to the shrine, strangely peaceful and even beautiful in the glimmer din with just a few children playing near the glass oratory. The statuary looked like white fish in an incandescent aquarium. Three women were sitting inside the glass walls looking up at Mary. One of them stepped forward and kneeled at Mary's feet. A lorry roared past. Car doors slammed.

I returned to the Basilica but, even in the encroaching darkness, it still failed to accrue much splendour. It aspired to the proportions of a cathedral yet had no cathedral atmosphere. But for the odd motifs of crosses carved into the walls – so crude they might have been medieval arrow slits – it could just have been any old pre-stressed concrete office block. It gave the unfortunate impression of being done on the cheap; even the tall spire was the colour of rust. It aspired without accomplishing; it had none of the authority that comes with age; it had no authenticity or intelligence.

Three women walked past arm in arm and humming. Everyone seemed happy and contented enough here, which was all that mattered, I guess. Even vulgarity can make people happier than small babies. Vulgarity can be fun though, for myself, I believe that vulgarity and holiness are inimical. Holiness loves the old, the regular and the unadorned which is strewn across the beaten path to our ancestors. Holiness makes worship a wondrously attractive love affair with God and draws people to it. Holiness sets up an argument so pure there is no rebutting it. Knock seemed to have no such qualities.

I walked back to the main road. That wandering bank of black cloud remained low and incredibly thick. Hardly anyone passed the oratory without stopping to look at the statuary and cross themselves. That man was still speaking loudly in the *Telefon* kiosk. A few midges bit into my neck like tiny stabs from sewing needles. A tractor rumbled down the road, headlamps blazing and trailer piled high with hay. There was that pungent aroma of burning peat and I knew I was back in my beloved Ireland again; back in the country which had given me so many hours of gurgling peace and happiness.

I hitch-hiked to Westport where I caught my first sight of Croagh Patrick, the highest mountain in Ireland. The Reek was

a huge black colossus shrouded in cloud and I had come to
climb it – along with some 40,000 other pilgrims – the following Sunday. Soon after undertaking the toughest pilgrimage in
the world at Lough Derg I was now about to tackle the highest.

Westport turned out to be a convivial jumble of terraced
houses, Wimpy bar and sawdust pubs scattered around a turbid
stream, thick with weeds and empty lemonade cans. It had
dowdy cafés, a church, shops bulging with postcards and sou-
venirs and a hotel with a tricolour and the stars and stripes
fluttering above its porch.

Around these hilly streets – where the faint but definite
whiff of the holiday camp came wafting around every corner
– everyone went very intently about their business. Within half
an hour I encountered a burly woman beggar with a baby in a
shawl and a gnarled hand permanently outstretched; an actor
who enthused all with his bar-room tales of the famous in New
York, home here to see his mother; two drunks who seemed to
be locked in an argument that was going to last a year and
countless men, with thick boots and caps set at jaunty angles,
sitting on walls and kicking their heels as they enjoyed the
crack.

The dark bars were alive with stumbling drunks with
Guinness stains down the front of their shirts; black-eyed
colleens who would show you the hem of their petticoats for
sixpence and wild, mad characters with raggedy, oily clothes
and billowing grey beards who played accordions in the often
forlorn hope of a free drink. Come 9.30 p.m. and the bars
filled up with folk bands – some good and some rotten – who
soon had the very sawdust dancing with their screeching Irish
music, screeching non-Irish music or, in one case, just plain
screeching which sent you running down the road with your
hands over your ears.

The Reek hovered over all this as proud and implacable as a
turbanned Sikh. Sometimes mists rose from the jagged slopes
as if they were on fire. If it was dark and damp The Reek
seemed to move away from the town, distant and sullen. If it
was fine the very mountain seemed about to stand on your foot.

Come to my slopes and I will teach you all about pain and outrage, The Reek seemed to be saying. Come to me all ye who are heavy laden and I will break your bones and your spirit and then, when you think you have nothing more to give, I will break your heart too.

So six o'clock came on the Saturday night before the great pilgrimage. I had climbed halfway up its slopes and was sitting in a bothy with just my sleeping bag, planning to spend the night on her rocks. By now a heavy rain was streaming down from the mountain's summit, gusting over the grey slopes and down onto the patchwork of fern and heather below. The polythene cover on my bothy was flapping around; shards of broken glass and hundreds of bottle tops were embedded in the earth floor. Perhaps I could have slept the night here, but somehow I did not fancy sleeping on all this glass, even if this was the only dry spot on the mountain.

They used to make this climb during the night but lately the church had ordered that it should be done at the crack of dawn. Yet even in this darkening drizzle some were already wending their way up the jagged path, a few in their bare feet.

Down below me the path twisted and turned until it reached the small village of Murrisk. Here, in a shop, a woman had loaned me a stick that would help me on the climb. Already the mineral water men and sellers of pious objects were setting up stalls at the bottom of the path, ready for the mob who would arrive early the next morning.

The view of the surrounding countryside from my bothy was quite staggering: a rolling, mist-shrouded vista of feudal Ireland, where peat bog sat next to mossy hummock and huge splintered meteors of rock lay scattered in the gorse. Even the sheep found it difficult to forage in this barren land and their ribs stuck out wretchedly. This was land which could not have changed one jot since St Patrick came up here and fasted for 40 days and nights while bargaining with God over the future security of the Irish.

Way out in front of me was Clew Bay with its 365 islands; one for each day of the year. The occasional upturned curragh lay on the grey shingle shore. A light wind blew bits of froth off the breeze-chopped sea, making them dance across the pebbles like stampeding candy floss. The gulls picked up the mussels and dropped the shells on the rocks to break them open.

I listened to the sounds of the mountain for a while, to the stream bursting with riotous laughter and the sticks of the pilgrims striking the stones as they made their way up the slopes. Their faces were red and blustery with the mounting cruelty of the weather. By now the rain was starting to sheet down something awful but even so I decided to stir my bones and make my way on up to the summit. It was one of my stupider decisions since quite soon I found my hands and feet scrambling on piles of wet, mossy rocks which wanted to dance as soon as I stepped on them. Visibility was but a few feet and the winds howled all around me. Occasionally the dark figure of a returning pilgrim emerged out of the dripping greyness and greeted me cheerily before disappearing in long, sliding crunches of stone.

I passed a few rubbled outbuildings and by now was thoroughly cowed since I had not seen anyone for at least half an hour, the rain had seeped right through my clothes and I had gashed my knee in a stumble. I could not decide if it was easier to carry on or go back. The sheer immensity of those slopes was so frightening – everything so savagely durable beneath my frail, panting, none-too-hardy body. I have been out of condition since the day I was born.

When I did stagger out onto the summit it was a strange and singular sight, curiously biblical with shivering donkeys standing next to piles of stones and makeshift stalls with men and boys huddled beneath tarpaulins like Bedouins in the windy desert as the rain continued sheeting down. The black shapes of a few pilgrims were doing their stations around and around a small cairn, known here as St Patrick's bed. Just along a bit was a tiny whitewashed chapel in which I sought shelter.

Inside a man was hammering together what looked like a communion rail with some five people sitting like penned cattle in small wooden stalls. I stripped off most of my wet clothes and dried myself with the inside of my sleeping bag, chatting with the man with the hammer, telling him what I was up to and whatnot. A writer out on his business of writing does well to ingratiate himself with whoever seems to be in charge. He was the chapel caretaker, he said, and he always came up here the night before the annual pilgrimage to make sure everything was all right.

More dripping, sodden figures came into the chapel and I spoke to two hotel girls from Castlebar who were busy demolishing a huge pile of sandwiches. So why had they come on this climb? 'Oh, that would be telling, wouldn't it?' one of them replied, giggling. There was a crusty old-timer from Westport who did not make too much sense and had been climbing up here every year since 1940. 'St Patrick brought the mountain here so we've got to look at it,' he said, straight-faced.

Gale-force winds kept bashing against the walls, demented, as we all settled down to spend the night in the chapel. I had never spent the night in any sort of church and certainly never expected that it would be as comfortless as this. Giant draughts came whistling in under every door and into the small main room. An altar cloth flapped around on a makeshift stand that looked suspiciously like a biscuit tin. Water poured down into butts in various places in the chapel, spilling over on the floor with a positively malevolent glee. The whole place stank of animal dung.

But anything – just anything – was better than being out in that storm and I was settling down in a dry, if smelly, corner of the chapel for a long night vigil when the caretaker announced the chapel was closing and everyone had to leave. Right in the middle of the night in the middle of the wildest storm! I could barely believe my ears. My mouth opened to squeak some sort of protest when he looked at me and said: 'You're all right. You can stay.'

His words were as welcome as a last-minute reprieve from the gallows and I could never remember feeling so relieved. It really does pay to ingratiate yourself with whoever is in charge. But my relief was tinged with strong edges of guilt nonetheless as the others picked up their belongings and walked out into that terrible storm. The caretaker locked the door behind them and now, where some 40,000 were expected, there was, for the moment, just one – me.

Sleep was out of the question as I stretched out on the cold hard floor in my sleeping bag, tennis shoes as a pillow, gazing up at the leaking chapel roof. My legs were stiff with the cramps and my knee was sore too as I tossed and turned. Every half an hour or so some pilgrim knocked on the door and cursed pitifully when he found it was locked.

Later it went quiet again. My consciousness was flickering between waking and sleeping when what sounded like a huge group turned up and began moving around the chapel chanting Hail Marys into the teeth of the storm. Around and around they went . . . *Hail Mary full of grace . . . blessed art thou amongst women . . . blessed is the fruit of your womb . . .* and even as I was stretched out on the chapel floor like a Plantagenet king on his tomb in the guttering darkness I saw, for the first time, what the bodies of the saints of old must have felt as they lay in state and pilgrims came from far and near to chant devotional prayers around them.

My eyes kept opening and closing when I just had to smile at the expanding absurdity of the whole notion. What would those sodden pilgrims have said, I wondered, if they had realized that, far from muttering prayers to their great Irish saint, they were in fact circling a damp Welsh bloke with a gashed knee lying in a sleeping bag in the darkness with a pair of tennis shoes as a pillow?

The prayers died away and the rains gradually ceased. But the winds kept pounding against the walls in the steady rhythm of breaking waves. Mighty winds are very evocative of the whirling mysteries of God, I think; so too are the summits of mountains where the imagination can liberate us from our puny forms and set us in a greater picture – way above the earth and resting in the hollow of the Lord's palm.

Singing rose up and died away in eddies. I dozed off and dreamed a strange dislocated dream of churches and chapels. I was wandering from altar to altar when I broke into a run ending up sliding across freezing ice. The ice cracked and I fell only to be held by the hand of Etheldreda herself. 'There's no milk for the tea,' she said softly before dropping me over a cliff from which I fell for all eternity.

With a sudden shuttling of bolts the caretaker opened the chapel door to let in as glorious a dawn as I have ever beheld; the rain and mist had been vanquished by a cool, ebullient sunshine with ravishing views of the Twelve Pins of Connemara, the scattered islands of Clew Bay and, beyond, the pine plantations approaching Donegal. Dotted over the brown patterned fields were cut turfs of peat stacked with such precision they might have been mysterious Druidical pyramids.

We were on the apex of a grey-green cone of rock. Sunshine swarmed down behind the clouds and anointed the heads of thousands of pilgrims who were making their way up the slopes. Many were barefoot, mud squeezing up between their toes, others in climbing boots and yet more in sandals. But all were smiling as they scrambled the last few yards to pay homage to their patron saint.

They might have been a medieval army on the march – a meandering crocodile stretching the three twisting miles down to Murrisk. All sorts of people came stumbling in with their hazel walking sticks: young girls in shorts, old women in long, black coats, men carrying small children on their shoulders, brawny men with delicate rosaries in their thick fingers, press photographers with cameras, mountain rescue men in white safety helmets and carrying stretchers to deal with broken ankles and crushed toes. Priests were among them, their working clothes tied up in a bundle as they toiled up the slopes to relieve the pressure on the others now taking confession in the chapel, dogs bounding around in the excitement of it all, mules hauling up yet more mineral water to sell at a pound a time. This ragged army was surging here for the first Mass of the morning.

I walked over to the other side of the chapel and bought a cup of tea off one of the Bedouins for a pound, not begrudging the price either, knowing what they had gone through in the night.

He told me to go and warm myself next to his peat fire where another man came and stood next to me. He had a face which looked as if he had been the victim of a thousand lost fights; his suit was torn and ripped. He said he had spent the night in the men's lavatory up here and kept shivering as he held his steaming mug of tea with both hands. I suspected he had got into a drunken brawl – something of a remarkable feat on a holy pilgrimage – but, try as I might, I could get no straight answers out of him.

Thin wisps of mist were chasing one another over the mountain. Already some 2,000 were surging around the chapel in the wiffling peat smoke. *Hail Mary full of grace* . . . And there it was again – the massed, marching, haunting music of the Irish at prayer. I worked my way back into the crowded chapel and listened to the service which was in Irish. Despite not understanding a word I was strangely lifted by the sheer effort which the pilgrims had made in getting here.

Later I went back down the slope feeling a sense of gladness as we descended into the gaudy circus of souvenir shops and mineral water men in Murrisk. Pop music was blaring out on a loudspeaker to attract people to a car raffle and already the pub was doing a roaring trade. But I was too exhausted for any merriment and returned to my hotel in Westport calculating that, by now, I had done enough penitential pilgrimage to sin, with impunity, until I dropped.

# 5

# The Fair Flower of Wales

HOLYWELL · ABERDARON · BARDSEY ·
LLANTWIT MAJOR · CHEPSTOW · TINTERN

The shrine effortlessly imprisoned you with the purity of its passion as soon as you stepped inside. It was something to do with the sweet cool shadows of the early morning and the carvings on the ageing stone pillars. It was also something to do with the centuries of prayer cobwebbed in the air. But most of all it was to do with the magic of the gorgeous morning sunlight sparkling on that spring water; the way light and water bubbled and swam together; the pure energy of that current bursting out of the smooth brown and green rocks. Yes, it was the water that best spoke of the pure passion of the place.

I had come early – just after eight in the morning – and changed into a bathing costume inside a canvas cubicle. I was still the only customer and my skin was goosepimpling riotously, more at the thought of what was to come than the warm reality of a midsummer morning. The water, the man in the ticket office told me, was as cold at this time of year as it was in the middle of winter, which was another way of saying it was very cold indeed all the year round.

Built directly over the well was a huge stone gazebo. Just next to it, right at my feet, was a long tank of cold water, large enough to hold four coffins piled up on top of one another, with an iron rail on either side. The gazebo, in its turn, was surrounded by an old stone chapel with fan vaulting and small, witty sculptures of little animals and flaking cheerful faces.

Many of the faces had been disfigured by the weather though one, facing me, was the perfectly distinguishable carving of one pilgrim carrying another through the pool on his back.

Just outside the building, in the dandelioned sunlight, was a small swimming pool with a few brown leaves skulling around on it like empty abandoned coracles. A huge stone sat on the floor of one side of the pool. St Bueno's stone.

I stared down at my reflection again, face featureless, legs white and arms holding my chest comfortingly. I placed my foot slowly in the water and took it out very quickly indeed. The water was so cold it was as if my foot had gone completely numb and I had to dance around the shrine, as if inventing a new one-legged waltz, before the blood got working through my frozen foot again. Somehow – and standing there at that moment I could not see how – I was going to have to get the whole of my body under that water and through that Arctic pit *three* times. I wished that I too had an obliging pilgrim to carry me through the water – someone tall enough that it meant only my knee-caps would be grazed by the freezing surface.

This was St Winefride's Well in Holywell, the Bethesda of North Wales and the most famous healing well in Wales. I was standing, my knees knocking, on a spot which was at the very heart of this great Celtic nation; a hallowed spot where the deaf came and first heard the bubbling of those holy waters; where the dumb found words of worshipful love flowing from their mouths; where the crippled abandoned their crutches and were able to dash across the fields outside; where the blind were first able to see and marvel at the lowering majesty of the nearby Snowdonia range.

Even in the violence-fouled days of the Reformation – when the shrine was locked up and broken down – pilgrims continued to come here, often at night and at considerable risk to their safety. Priests conducted services in disguise and even when threatened with the dungeon, sword and stake pilgrims kept coming, making this well the only place of unbroken pilgrimage since the seventh century.

I dipped my big toe into the water again and found it every bit as cold as I had first feared. Behind me was a stone statue of St Winefride – 'The fair flower of Wales, hope of distressed pilgrims and patron saint of Holywell.' She had a crook in one hand and the palm of martyrdom in the other. A stone gown flowed around her shoulders with a crown on her head. Yet it was the thin white line around her neck which told her story; a tale as mysterious and inherently improbable as the fare structure of British Rail.

We must go back to one morning in November 660 when Caradoc, a Welsh prince from Hawarden returned, hot and lusty, after being out hunting. The beautiful, if cool, Winefride sparkled his sexual fancy and he made overtures, only to be firmly rebuffed. In a rage he pursued her, sword in hand, and as she ran seeking the sanctuary of the church, he hacked her head clean off her body.

At that moment Winefride's uncle, St Bueno, emerged from the church and laid the curse of God on the murderer, whereupon the earth opened and swallowed up Caradoc. This well also sprang up from where Winefride's head rolled. But the miracles did not end there. The old saint prayed the girl's life would be restored and, lo, he placed her head back on her body and life returned to her. But a line remained around her neck for the rest of her life which she spent as a nun in a community at Gwytherin.

It is another of those stories with very little sex but plenty of violence which has come down to us from medieval times. Perhaps it is best seen as an illustration of the great dignity of women in medieval Wales; a parable of the inviolable role she played in the family and the dispensation of hospitality to strangers. She could never be struck or insulted but a husband could strike her lightly below her shoulders if she gave away his harp, cloak or cauldron. 'Oh darling, you haven't given the cauldron away again have you?'

So when Caradoc sought to ravish her, he was striking at the open hospitality which was the peculiar glory of early Welsh life. When he attacked her he was attacking the whole idea of womanhood and his actions were motivated by lust, the hall-mark of the barbarian who would deny the Welsh their right to enter the kingdom of God – or so the Celtic theorists of old would have seen it.

When I finally dropped my body into the water I must have frozen a good year's growth out of it. My bones seemed to be breaking into dust and I squealed out loud. The cold pounded my shoulders and thumped down on my head. My chest tight-ened alarmingly and when I scrambled out on the other side my body had lost all feeling. I danced around the gazebo until the blood began flowing again. My skin was all goosepimples and blue patches. And I had to do it all twice more.

I expected my second immersion would be easier but I was wrong. Whole sections of my body fell into a frozen coma; thin shrieks of agony wriggled out between my teeth. On the third dip I did not think I was going to make it through the trough at all. A rage of purple agony skewered me and I would have told the torturer anything – anything at all – he wanted to know. I certainly did not pause to pray in the water as you are supposed to.

Just then another pilgrim came out of the cubicle, went straight down into the water, bobbed up his head, held up his hands together in prayer, kissed the stone on the side of the trough and walked up the stone steps. 'Lovely that was,' he told me. 'It was really cold yesterday.'

My amazed eyebrows shot straight into my hairline. 'What do *you* call cold then?' I asked.

'This is warm. Smashing this is. You could sleep in this.'

He went down into the water for a second time and again said an interminable prayer. After his third dip he got out and went over to the swimming pool where he knelt by the large stone, saying another prayer with just his head sticking up out of the water. It is said St Bueno sat on this stone when he was instructing Winefride.

His name, I discovered, was Kosta Nedic, a cheerful Yugo-slavian Catholic with thermal skin and fur-lined bones who made his living laying tarmacadam. His mother-in-law had been cured in this well – 'She left her wheelchair behind' – and he visits it whenever he can. 'See here,' he said, pointing at the steps going down into the well. 'Every year, on the anniversary of Winefride's death, those steps drip with blood. I've not seen it myself but that's what they say. Just under the water-line there.'

He towelled his bushy hair and eyebrows. 'I've been coming here most of my life. There used to be crutches and surgical boots the cured left behind. But there's nothing like that around now, is there? It's the young isn't it? The young have lost their faith.'

A lad in torn jeans with a large gold ear-ring came into the shrine and filled up a petrol can with water. He had driven here from Worcestershire. 'Mum likes to have it around the house. If any of the kids get sick she showers them with it.'

A few more came in. An Irish lad borrowed ten pence off me to light a votive candle and two very dubious characters, with dirty, oil-stained jackets and in dire need of a shave, proceeded to fill up empty whisky and cider bottles. Was there something alcoholic about the water I didn't know about? The elder of the two men screwed up his whisky bottle carefully and explained the water had once cured him of soft legs when he was but four years old. The Irish lad, who had borrowed ten pence off me, now wanted to borrow my bathing costume so he could do the three-fold dip.

'They're all bums,' Kosta whispered into my ear fiercely. 'Wherever you go you can't get away from bums. Even in a holy place like this. Bums.'

A van pulled up outside and what seemed like hundreds of kids dashed into the shrine, stripped off their clothes and began splashing around in the St Bueno's pool. The man in charge of them had the swarthy good looks of a Romany. 'I'm a traveller, sir. Move about a bit, you know.'

The laughter and splashes of the children somehow went well with the spirit of prayer in the place; the shrieks of the young rising to mingle with the prayers for the dead – an odd little conjunction for sure, as mysterious and joyful as a rock 'n' roll party in a church crypt.

But the shrine curator did not find it remotely joyful and quickly shooed the children out. 'This is not a swimming pool,' he told the Romany fiercely. 'This is a holy shrine.'

I thought it was a shame the children were kicked out of the water which they were clearly enjoying. Places of prayer should be places of fun too and I rather fancy old Bueno would have loved watching those children play. He wasn't one of those crusty old saints who never changed his boots from one Easter to the next. He was a funny, bold man, challenger of tyrants and a friend of the helpless. And anyone who set about trying to convert the difficult and obdurate peoples of North Wales must have had a great sense of humour.

Then it was Sunday morning and we were all huddled together in a small fishing boat as it chugged out over the softly swelling waves from the village of Aberdaron on Lleyn Peninsula, making our way to Bardsey, the sacred island of Wales.

Aberdaron was a raggle-taggle of white-washed houses flung down in front of a sandy beach and around a gull-sentinelled chapel. Indeed the only feature of the village that seemed to have any symmetry was the graveyard with its lines of grey slate tombstones, as formal as parade-ground soldiers, marching line by line up a grassy incline. Otherwise the village was a ragged gathering of shop, pub and inn around a stone bridge with, at the centre, a small white tea-house known as The Big Kitchen where pilgrims of old, about to make the trip over to Bardsey and waiting for suitable weather, could claim a free meal. Not free any longer, of course: 50p for a cup of tea and up to three or four pounds for such as scampi or steak and chips.

Our boat bucked as the sea swelled and the row-boat we were towing behind us yawed wildly. We were now passing cormorant cliffs leading up to uncompromising headlands, barren of trees and dotted with mounds of spiky gorse the shape and size of giant pumpkins. On the other side of the bay a whole gabbling gale of herring gulls were swooping in and out of the sea.

There might have been 500 of those infernal gulls who had been creating the most hellish racket in the bay for the last four days as they fluttered above and dived into a shoal of whitebait who, in their turn, had been trying to escape from a shoal of mackerel. It was clearly no fun being a whitebait, harassed from above and behind, and neither was it much fun listening to the cries and screams of those gulls. They had kept me awake all night in my hotel bedroom on the beach. One second their calls were slow asthmatic gasps which built up in intensity and frequency until they changed abruptly into the crazed shrieking laughter of witches happily despatching their enemies with pins in dolls.

'That's St Mary's Well there,' said one of our group pointing at a wave-lapped headland. 'It's got a fresh water spring which is covered by the tide. But the water always stays fresh and the Bardsey pilgrims used to use it. One of the Lord's miracles to help pilgrims on their way, they say.'

There were twelve of us travelling across the Sound that morning: Menna Hughes, a woman who had once farmed on the island and was today going back for the first time for years; a Scottish couple on holiday in nearby Pwllheli; a couple from Kingston-on-Thames; a man on holiday from his work in a creamery and an elderly lady who had once taught on the island for five years. We also had three children with us, all led by our skipper Huw Williams, a bulky man with Shredded Wheat muscles and sprayed-on shorts. He sported a denim cap made in the People's Republic of China and I dubbed him Captain Birds Eye.

'Terrible storms there were when we were on the island,' Menna recalled. 'We could get caught out for five or six weeks without a boat of any kind. Terrible it was. We'd run low on flour we would – all kinds of things went short. We'd go over the cliffs to get gulls' eggs to eat. What were they like? I'll tell you. They had a dark yolk and weren't very nice at all.'

We turned around the headland and I caught my first sight of Bardsey. As impressive as a good punch in the mouth it was too, a huge volcanic fist of jagged rocks, some a sooty black and others as red as rust. One side of the island rose up mountainously with a thick tablecloth of mist lying around its summit while, on the other end, sat the white tower of a Trinity lighthouse. A cormorant flew past us, its neck as straight as a spear.

'See that rock there?' said Menna. 'They used to send messages from there to the mainland if they wanted anything. They had to light a flash, they did.'

Yes, it was clear I had found yet again a place set apart; that special isolation of spirit which I had found in Iona and Lindisfarne; that quality of inviolate purity which is the essential quality of a holy place.

A religious house was first set up on this island in 480 by Cadfan, the patron saint of warriors. By the Middle Ages the island had become a great religious centre; something of what Iona was to Scotland. People wanted to die and be buried here to such an extent the island became known as the Island of the Twenty Thousand Saints. Pilgrims came here from all over Europe and Pope Calixtus II – 'in view of the perilous nature of the trip to Rome' – declared that three pilgrimages to Bardsey would, in future, be counted as equal to one pilgrimage to Rome.

But this same Pope, who also declared that two pilgrimages to St David's was worth one to Rome, was not the thoughtful, avuncular type we have today but an irritable old bore who kept dreaming up these formulae because he wanted to thin out the intolerable throng of pilgrims who kept jamming up the streets and hostels of his beloved Rome.

The Bardsey pilgrimage ended in the Reformation and the monastery here was pillaged. Later the island was taken over by farmers and, for one period, became a hang-out for pirates. The island even had its own kings and when the last one, King Love Pritchard, turned up at the Eisteddfod he was welcomed by

David Lloyd George as one of those Welsh 'from overseas'. These days there was just a hermit, a Franciscan monk, a tiny community based on a farm and a bird sanctuary.

Captain Birds Eye rowed us alongside a small concrete jetty where a few launches lay on their sides and lobster pots were piled up high next to a shed. I struck out straight for the old Augustinian Abbey since I wanted to catch the service there that morning. Hurrying along the dirt path with alarmed rabbits dashing away from me and straight down their holes, my heart was soon gliding on strong emotional breezes of happiness again. I stopped still a few times, smiling at the sun and warmed right through in the way you get when you suddenly realize that someone, somewhere in the world is praying for you. There really was healing magic in the air on that island and I could have all but shouted out with joy, renewed in the feeling of the closeness of the resurrection in the morning; in the certainty that the new will always be born out of the ashes of the old.

Everything about the morning was lovely. Being surrounded by water. The pleasing tidiness of the fields shorn of all spare grass by the foraging sheep and rabbits. The grey stone cottages. The snatched sounds of hymnody being born aloft and shaken around by the sun-drenched winds. Forever enchanting to the Welsh ear are such sounds which, like the smell of roast beef and the theme tune of 'Family Favourites', tell of all those plump Sundays of our childhoods when we lay around eating too much, listening to the radio as Mam washed up the dishes and worrying that, one day, she would stop loving us and run off somewhere.

I only caught the final notes of the last hymn of the service though what could be a more beautiful setting for any act of worship than this ancient rubble with the call of the birds in the rafters of a great blue sky, surrounded by, on one side, Anglesey, just here the mighty sweep of Cardigan Bay and, way over the sea, the Wicklow mountains in Ireland? The small congregation filed out through the graveyard where, on a huge Celtic cross, there was the telling inscription: 'Is it nothing to you, all ye who pass by?'

When all of them had left I introduced myself to Brother Nathanael, a Franciscan friar who said that, as soon as he had changed out of his vestments, he would take me down to his house for a cup of coffee. He was here for the summer to look after pilgrims and seemed positively abrim with the love and gaiety of his spiritual leader, St Francis.

As we were going back along the path to his house a woman came walking across a field towards us. She moved as slowly as a publisher's decision, with tiny stooped shoulders, fingers bent with arthritis and a black cowl over her head. She smiled, showing a few gold teeth below a simply enormous beak of a nose and the large, sad brown eyes of a boxer dog. 'Your visitor might like this,' she said in a voice so soft you could barely hear it as she handed Nathanael a leaflet entitled *Tramping Down Death by Death*. 'You are both well I hope.'

With this, and before we could say anything, she left us as softly and slowly as she had come. She was Sister Helen Mary, the hermit on the island. She spoke rarely and survived on a small vegetable patch and a lot of prayer, Nathanael explained. She was one of the Sisters of the Love of God and had been living in the loft of some old stables for ten years now. If Nathanael ever complained to her about anything her reply was always the same; 'Pray, brother, just pray. Nothing else matters.'

As he made the coffee, Nathanael admitted he did not know much about modern things. 'When I first came here no one had a fridge. There was no electricity, just calor gas lamps, candles or torches.' He also had the tattiest gown I have ever seen – all patches and stitches with so many rips it would have been rejected by an Oxfam shop on a slow day. 'It's my second best,' he said when I asked if the vow of poverty meant just one gown until you died. 'I was going under some barbed wire the other day and tore the sleeve here. I fear it's on its last legs now.'

We talked of the island and he smiled as he said it really was possible that 20,000 had been buried here. Wherever you dug there were masses of bones. 'Any historical journal will tell you that all along the coast right down to Aberystwyth, people always asked to be buried here. They would even have makeshift mortuaries where they stored the bodies if the weather was too bad to get over to the island.'

Nathanael was an Anglican Franciscan who tried to welcome every pilgrim to the island in the summer. At that moment he was friary-less since his last friary had been closed down, but at the end of that summer he was going to be based in Llandudno as a part-time priest. Much of his time on the island was spent in prayer: morning compline, midday office and evening prayer. Prayer, you sensed, provided him with the pattern of fidelity crucial to his love of the Lord. In a way his life was one long, secret prayer.

Being a good Franciscan he loved the profusion of birds and rabbits. He was saddened when myxomatosis struck the island and many of the rabbits had died. Only that morning he had seen one such rabbit with its face swollen up and blind, bumping wretchedly against a stone wall. Even as he spoke, his gentle radiance told me much about the practice and presence of God. He was one of those rare and valuable men who mediate the idea of God to us; a simple, good man in whom you can find the very icon of the risen Christ. We spoke for a while about another good man I knew: Canon David Watson, the great York evangelist who had recently been stricken by cancer. Then we sat around a table and prayed for David's recovery; that God would send his angels to kiss the disease out of David's body; that he would be fully restored to us and the Church.

It was one of those prayers in which we had all entered into a dialogue with the power of healing Love. When we had finished it, there was nothing more to say.

Over the hills and out to sea they drifted. Yellow-bellied from the rising sun they went one by one and two by two, hurrying along with the winds, being shunted to wherever clouds are shunted before they fade away and are no more. Above them the long vapour trails of climbing jets sliced up the grey-blue dawn into giant white squares, bisected here and there by the endless caravan of those clouds . . . four, five, six . . . eleven, twelve, thirteen . . . marvellous fluffy frontrunners in a floating marathon across the heavens.

Autumn was foreclosing on the summer with the dark nights drawing in when I came to Llantwit Major, a small town in the Vale of Glamorgan, to resume my search for holiness. It was a time of earwigs and the sudden rifle shots of cooking apples in the orchards. Gardeners were out lighting bonfires and scraping up the first of the dead leaves into dank piles. The tomato plants were withering in the greenhouses and, everywhere, there were lots of daddy long legs, all spindly limbs and tiny black bodies, looking menacing as they lurked around in porches, like plain-clothes men trying, but failing, to look unobtrusive.

This morning, standing counting the clouds out in the village streets, the very rooftops were singing with the kiss of an Indian summer which had come bragging to the yellowing leaves on the trees, making the morning dew sparkle as she glided her magisterial way from lane to lane, as gorgeous as a queen on her way to her coronation.

Only the postman and milkman were up and about their business: the rest of the village snoozed on behind drawn curtains. The pubs scattered around the stone monument in the square were as closed and still as hangovers. Just a few tiny snails with delicate white and red shells were out strolling over the pavements. Johnny Jones's cockerel greeted the dawn with a few thin calls but there was none of the cockerel's normal jubilant exuberance since, as Johnny Jones now says, the bird is nearly 14 years old and full of sleep. Many in the village were looking forward to the day the bird went to sleep for good.

St Illtyd founded the first university in Britain here in Llantwit. As saints go, St Illtyd was pretty much second division but his achievements were still considerable. Not only did he perform miracles (when thieves stole his pigs he turned them into stone which is no mean miracle by any standards) but he also clearly had a brain the size of a garage: 'Now this Illtyd was the most learned of all Britons in his knowledge of the Scriptures, both the Old and New Testaments and in every branch of philosophy, poetry and rhetoric, grammar and arithmetic;

and he was most wise and gifted with the power of foretelling future events.'

He also had the typical medieval saint's rapport with animals. Once, upset by the constant cries of crows, he gathered them together in his church and imposed a vow of silence on them. He also gave shelter to a stag fleeing from King Meridian and, thereafter, the stag stayed with him.

But his greatest glory was his university. Three thousand students were here, accommodated in seven halls. Eight hundred small wooden cells were built on this spot – this most beautiful of places, as St Illtyd's biographer called it, surrounded by the ditch and mound which comprised the Llan or sacred enclosure. They built a tiny wooden church for prayer and meditation and instituted the old monastic rules of *Laus Perennis* – praise without end. The students were divided into 24 groups with each group responsible for one hour of worship and adoration, ensuring that ceaseless praise ascended to God around the clock.

All types of people came here to study the great truths: scholars and poets, ecclesiastics and missionaries, beggars and royalty. There were even three saints here from Brittany – Samson of Dol, Gildas and Paul Aurelian – who, in their turn, spread the news of Illtyd's work throughout their own country to the extent that we still find Illtyd's name attached to many Breton churches.

St David also studied here and the story goes that one of his teachers, Paulinus, had lost his sight and though many had looked at his eyes none could understand the reason for his affliction. Only David would not look since, he said, he had never raised his eyes to his master's face. Paulinus praised his humility but asked David to touch his eyes and, when David finally agreed, the old teacher could see again.

Some say St Patrick – or Maenwyn as he was called in Welsh – was studying in one of these classrooms when the place was invaded by a gang of Picts and he was taken off as a slave to Slemish. But apart from all these stories there is now hardly any evidence of St Illtyd's old university of the saints. It survived up to the Norman conquest but little remains apart from the memorial stones and crosses in the church itself, all carved with characteristic Celtic interlacing designs.

I was sitting in the pews that afternoon when I heard squirrel-like noises coming from behind the organ and found it was an amiable old man, Ernest Brook, setting up his gear to photograph a tombstone built into the wall. He had an extremely small head with gaunt skeletal features and, although a retired teacher, he was, he said, spending his remaining years studying old churches. 'I collect tombstones the way other people collect old violins.' He then launched into a vivid and robust lecture on the place, pulling up carpets and pushing aside cupboards, his mouth a veritable machine gun of knowledge and insight.

'You can see that this gravestone in the chancel must be about 1624. We know that because the cross went out in that year. And look here. Two brothers dying on the same day, Christmas Day, in 1756. That must be unusual. See this. The mason couldn't fit in his lettering so he jammed it all in here. Why didn't he chalk it out first? You tell me. This man would have been put in there the year Walter Raleigh was executed. I've been studying this other stone for some time. The problem is the Latin is wrong. They had to strain the grammar to get it to fit. This tombstone says he was one hundred and twenty-nine when he died. It is clearly a lie. He might have been twenty-nine and some eighteenth-century vandal added the one. It's nice to think they had their own vandals too. I love this one. See the crudity of the lettering . . .'

And so this amiable and engaging crank went on, making me realize how superficial my examination of many churches had been; how these places had evolved over the centuries in a way which meant that every corner had its own story which it yielded up only too happily to a little study and thought.

The old market town of Chepstow is built on a great cliff rising out of the west bank of the River Wye, as you can see immediately you get off the bus there. All the streets slope so steeply it's a wonder they don't use the place as a forcing ground for mountaineers. One is even called Steep Street. I looked around this strange wonky jumble with shops, gabled houses and old buildings. It has a leisure centre and a bingo hall. There is also a huge stone gate over the main road which has been bashed and dented by a century of traffic. The ancient tribe of Silures built the earthworks of the town, the Romans fortified it, the Saxons traded in it, the Normans built a castle on it and now Chepstow has the slightly pained air of distressed country gentlefolk, broken down by the twin perils of traffic and the twentieth century but, somehow, managing to hang onto a few vestiges of dignity and self-respect.

There wasn't a bus to Tintern for another two hours so I decided to walk there, following the road out past the race-course and keeping a watchful eye on a spaniel who, in his turn, was keeping a watchful eye on me. But there was no attack and I trudged along a grass verge down into the wooded valley quite happily, whistling to myself and the falling leaves.

They were as grand as I hoped they would be, those falling leaves, drifting across the road in clouds of brown confetti and crunching under my feet. Leaves drifted past me in ones, twos and rattling storms. Leaves went tumbling over the road like acrobats; I could hear them scratching on the surface as they went, soft but distinct like the faint rasp of fingernails on black-boards, many suddenly dancing demented jigs in the draughts of passing cars as yet another breeze shook loose another crackling shower of leaves across my path.

A helicopter chattered overhead and hundreds of black-headed gulls stood around in a field, all facing the wind, as motionless and formal as a wartime cemetery. On one bend in the road I stood on the bank of a pond watching a duck when, in a furious flutter of wings, another duck broke cover from the reeds near my feet and they both flew off for some peace and quiet. Everywhere there was that rich, yeasty smell of autumn; that lovely fat scent which so perfectly describes a season putting up the shutters and closing down for winter.

The woods thickened and moved away in misty banks – here

a despondent and dead elm; out there a green line of Christmas trees wading down through a sea of brown. A magpie went foraging through the bare branches and, faraway, I could hear the aggrieved clinking of a blackbird. When the breezes stopped twirling the remaining leaves on the branches the woods were as fresh and still as a mountain tarn, the giant creepers curling everywhere.

I was walking on down the road picking some leaves out of my collar when I glimpsed the River Wye winding along the valley floor. I continued moving along the road, sipping on a can of lemonade. Another clearing, and there was Tintern Abbey. It was the strangest sensation: the first flash of a lovely dream and my heart was smitten with delight. I just stopped walking and said 'Oh boy' softly to myself, standing there on the side of the road while looking down at this incredible ruin, squatting on a flat tableau at the bottom of the valley, guarded by the river and framed by a huge orb of pale shimmering sunshine and autumnal wood.

Although it had no roof the abbey was almost a complete building, sitting there, disdainful in its own majesty, serene in the mellow certainty that comes to the very old. I understood immediately the power of its charm; the way it attracted painters and poets to those 'bare ruin'd choirs where late the sweet birds sang' with those rows of gaping glassless windows and the great seven-light window on the west wall, standing erect up against the sky like a huge pair of closed pincers.

The ruin now attracted some hundred thousand visitors a year and I was but one more plodding down the hill, through a cloud of whirling gnats, in search of somewhere to spend the night. A shopkeeper directed me up a back lane to a bed and breakfast and very pleasant it was too, run by Barbara, a handsome Welsh lady with big eyes and a soft heart who not only talked too much but knew she talked too much. 'When you've had enough just walk away. I won't mind.'

Later I took dinner in the Anchor Hotel; a wondrous melange of the old and new, somehow exactly summing up what a modern pilgrim might expect to find when he came to pay homage to those beautiful, mad Cistercian monks who first built the abbey here in 1130.

In the bar there was an old cider press with a huge stone wheel sitting next to one of those one-armed bandits with PRESS and HOLD and so many lights and buttons you needed an electronics degree to figure out how it worked. Taped muzak percolated through speakers somewhere in the black wooden rafters. But nothing would prepare the modern pilgrim for the menu. It was unique in my travels. Starters were described as Matins. You could choose between *Holy Order*, a 'bowl of homemade soup fit for a serf'; *Abbot Wyche*, a prawn cocktail, or *Nicolaus of Llandaff*, fried scampi.

Then there was The Feast itself: *Catherine of Aragon*, grilled fillet steak; *Jane Seymour*, grilled T-bone steak; *Anne Boleyn*, scampi provençale; *The Reformation Charter*, grilled lemon sole; *Thomas Cromwell*, succulent sirloin steak and *William Wordsworth*, salmon from the Wye poached in white wine. For Compline you could have *Cistercian Rites*, once known as profiteroles or *Tynterne Order*, which turned out to be homemade apple pie. The special liqueur coffees came as *Cromwell's Conquest* with cognac; *Wolsey's Wallop*, with whisky; *Raleigh's Ruin* with Tia Maria or *Cardinal's Nightcap*, simply coffee.

I ordered a *Holy Order* with a medium-rare *Catherine of Aragon* followed by a *Cistercian Rites* and a large *Cardinal's Nightcap*. Despite the curious nomenclature it was delicious and beautifully presented. I later discovered I had caused something of a panic in the kitchen since the barmaid had spotted me making notes on the menu and everyone had assumed I was an Egon Ronay inspector. 'We've only just applied and thought you were the man,' said the landlady. 'A right old fuss you caused.'

Later that night I went back to the abbey ruin. Its spiky towers stretched up against the darkening blue of the evening, spectral, black and holy. It is said that, by night, you can hear the Gregorian chants of the long-dead monks in those ruins but, standing there with my hands on the railings, all I could hear were the faint sounds of birds roosting and burbling in the rafters. There were all sorts of birds in there, I had learned, mostly racing pigeons who had dropped out on their ways home. I must say I loved the idea of a drop-out pigeon, a sort of cosmic cowboy of the skies, who decided that he'd had enough of this pointless racing lark and merely wanted to spend the rest of his days in this majestic ruin.

Through each window I could see the star-smattered sky while the air was wet with river mists and the faintest taste of woodsmoke. I was peering through the encroaching darkness at the twin doorway and some of the elaborate wall panels when a car came along the main road, its headlamps slicing through the trees and rolling over the giant pincers of the west wall, making them shiver and dance like something erupting out of a giant firework. Then everything went dark and quiet again and I put my hands in my pockets.

Far away there was the shrieking commotion of farmyard animals. Down by the Anchor Hotel red and yellow flushes of neon glowed on the dark river as it flowed silently about its river business.

# 6

## Lost on the Old Way

ISLE OF WIGHT · WINCHESTER · AYLESFORD ·
CANTERBURY

It was early evening and raining on the castellated, red-brick spires of Quarr Monastery on the Isle of Wight. The rain was tadpoling down the leaded windows with the wind pounding against the doors and walls. Suddenly, two soft chimes of bells hung in the weeping night. Yet, inside the monastery walls, there was a silence which swept all around; it moved through the darkened crypt, hung around the pointed arches of the cloisters and was all but deafening in the high wide church lit by just one guttering candle. Another few bells.

Doors opened around the cloisters and men in black, billowing robes slipped silently down to the refectory. It was time for the 7.30 supper and, after bowing to the figure of Christ pinioned to the walls, some 23 of them stood behind wooden chairs as one led the Grace and the others responded. They took their knives and forks out of huge, white linen napkins which they stuffed into their collars and ate a plain meal of beetroot, scrambled egg and bread. In the glimmering half-light they made no sound – apart from the scrape of cutlery on plates – and sat three or four feet away from one another.

Many were old, grey and balding; some had ruddy faces and others were pasty with more than a few being young men, short of hair and with bright, animated movements. A man in a small, brick pulpit – according to the Benedictine rule – read a book as they ate. The reading was slow and incantatory.

Tonight it was the story of Orione, a man who had just been beatified.

They ate fast since they didn't want to keep anyone else waiting. First and last this was a community of men in which sensitivity to one another was finely honed. Yet the brevity and simplicity of the meals were very much a part of the lifestyle of Quarr – perhaps the most simple and unadorned life to be found anywhere in Britain.

After a short period of recreation more bells heralded the start of Compline or evening prayer. Within these walls bells were the music of the nights and days. They struck off the hours and announced the beginning and end of prayers. We heard tiny tinkling bells, fat, echoing bells and huge romping gongs which bounced right down to the very foundations of the crypt.

I had come by train to Portsmouth, crossing on the ferry to Ryde where I took a taxi to this strange place and had been welcomed by these pained, unworldly men who were afraid of cameras, unwilling to look you directly in the eye and only spoke when spoken to and then with a great deal of effort.

Compline was a sight of religious beauty, stirring the spirit and the eye. The robed monks took their places in the choir stalls and almost immediately the lights were turned out with but one burning candle. As they chanted and knelt before God, their black, rounded shapes revolved around and dissolved into one another in the flickering light. Their voices, amplified by the empty nave, were astonishingly strong as the Gregorian chants carolled out, sometimes in unison and sometimes duelling as the sacred mysteries were celebrated. Finally the Abbot sprinkled holy water over all as a purification. Catch a drop on your cheek and it seemed to burn.

At nine came The Great Night Silence when all that could be heard was the wind hurtling around the monastery walls and shaking the branches of the pine trees in the gardens. *May the Lord grant us a quiet night and a perfect end.*

Even in the night silence there were still tiny bells ringing soft and sweet, redolent with the jubilation of Christmas carols.

And the wind kept sighing in the pines until, at 5 a.m., the cloister bells pealed out again, fat and assertive, stirring the monks out of their slumbers in readiness for Matins, which is the only service of the day in which they don their hoods. This is the coldest time of day and the Benedictine tradition holds that a donned hood reinforces the desired feeling of isolation and oneness with God alone. It is a service of psalms, hymns and scripture reading.

In the half an hour between Matins and Lauds, Dom Matthew Taylor has a period of silent prayer in his room. The monastic life, he told me, was one long process of coming close to God. 'Yet the closer you come, the further away God seems to be. He is nothing like his created reality. The more you understand the more you realize you don't understand. He is only like himself.'

These are mystical, lonely thoughts, though in the constant cycle of prayers, silences and chants in this stone place, you sense something of the mystical, lonely search for God. In the steady, almost punishing rhythm of their days you sense the barren loneliness of the wilderness into which Christ was driven to overcome the blandishments of Lucifer and grow in his isolation in his knowledge of God.

Here too the doors were being constantly locked to protect the monks from outside interference; bolted to allow them the tranquillity in which their faith could grow. There was no television or radio to poison their ideas.

Father Joseph Warrilow, whose long fingers wove and shaped the air as he spoke, has been a monk for 54 years, 33 of them here. He confessed to great difficulty in learning to love God, even though he knew God loved him. 'The Psalms give such a mixed picture of God. Perhaps I haven't given it enough time.' He did once have a mystical experience when he was shaving, he said, when he *knew* he was one of God's creatures. 'Many believe life here is too ceremonialized, but we shouldn't change it. Life becomes more and more an act of faith. Most of us have come through some kind of crisis. You learn to feel truth. If you can feel it you know it to be true. Our days are much the same as they were in medieval times and we must keep witness to faith when so many others are losing theirs.'

Quarr was now around half full since they were short of the right men with sufficient sympathy for Benedictine ideals. One such right man was Brother Denis Bradley who had been here for seven years. 'Yes, I feel quite well absorbed now,' he told me. 'I don't believe I'll ever leave.'

The base of the monastery is academic, rather than physical, and Brother Denis tried to spend at least three hours a day studying theology with a view to becoming a priest. He enjoyed the full balance of the monastic day and actually laughed a lot which came as something of a surprise since most of the others were solemn, serious men. They own nothing at all – even their clothes are given to them. 'But we've really got quite a lot.' That laugh again.

Outside in the monastery grounds a brown, brackish sea lapped against a beach littered with debris and driftwood. A car tyre waltzed around in the waves and a tree had fallen over. Some monks were working in the gardens, a few chopping wood. They try to grow as much of their own food as they can. Those bells floated in the damp breeze again.

The centrepiece of the day was the full Mass and Communion in the middle of the morning. The monks wore bright red robes and walked into the church chanting together. Just before Communion they all hugged and kissed one another to underline their brotherhood.

Here, surely, was the real meaning of holiness: men prepared to endure any hardship or sacrifice to break down the barriers to their relationship with the King; men righteous, just and fearful of the holy wrath of God which is the beginning of all wisdom; men loving one another and weaving a great web of prayer for the world with Christ at its heart.

These holy men were fulfilling a contract with God. They were giving him the prayer he loves to hear and, in so doing, trying to save the world from drifting into a new Dark Age. Perhaps they could see a time when God, in his rejected and disappointed wrath, would send in floods and tempests that might last for years, when people on those darkling deserts would be forever lost and crying out with pain since they could no longer even touch those they loved.

These men – like Columba, Aidan, David, Patrick and Dunstan before them – were giving up their lives that others could keep theirs. They were keeping the flames of love alight at a time when an ocean of cold evil was flooding every corner of the world. Theirs was real faith. Theirs was real sacrifice. Theirs, surely, was the true path of holiness.

It was winter when I got off the train in Winchester to resume my journey. Squalls of acid rain came sweeping in over the station car park and a man suffering from gargoylism walked past. Bodies were bent low, struggling against the squalls and, up near the shopping centre, a bearded tramp was sheltering in the doorway. He was muttering evilly to himself, his possessions tied up with string and newspapers, scattered around his feet. A green bus roared past, smashing up the carefully composed rain puddles and making them leap around in angry grey sprays.

It was the coldness of the wind which was the worst, slicing through your trousers and making you grit your teeth and whistle thinly at the sheer discomfort of it all. The wind made great polythene sheets flap around noisily on a building site in front of the cathedral. Occasionally a bird broke free in the wild skies or a crouching figure dashed across the cathedral lawns and disappeared through a stone arch. Yet, even in the cold rain, the cathedral looked mountainous, spine-chilling, infused with the careful craftsmanship of centuries.

All those cold and bare tree branches lashing the air forlornly seemed to suit Winchester. This was the most ancient and austere of cities. You saw its tremendous age in the buildings leaning at crazy angles and the exposed half-timberings on the house fronts. The winding streets and old stone walls spoke of antiquity. It might even have been built old, sprawling around, as it was, with its empty spaces full of rain and the mocking calls of rooks.

We were 120 miles from Canterbury and I had come to walk The Old Road between these two ancient cities: a meandering, disappearing track hallowed by centuries of travel and the foot-steps of millions of pilgrims who had started their journey here after sailing into Southampton. They had first taken this road – The Pilgrim's Way – to pay tribute to Thomas à Becket after he was murdered in Canterbury Cathedral in 1170.

It soon became clear that the cathedral authorities here were anxious to speed me on my way. The dean refused to see me, say-ing he was about to go on holiday. The verger had retired the week before. I asked a woman a question outside and she said 'I don't know' and walked away. The welcome in the cathedral itself was not exactly joyful either. A forest of placards suggested I cough up some money and a black-coated attendant stood next to a collection box, wearing a mugging smile. The lady in the cathedral shop was a treasure of frostiness. Oh yes, she knew absolutely hundreds of super people who knew all kinds of things about pilgrimage but none who'd welcome me knocking on their door. Oh no. Absolutely not. This was Winchester. People had to make proper appointments in Winchester.

Totally discouraged I knocked it all on the head and went to see a James Bond film in the local cinema.

The next morning I returned to the cathedral and, unable to take any further off-handedness, let the building do the talking. It was indeed lovely and ravishing. The sheer height and splendour of the nave – with twelve bays, the largest Gothic nave in the world, they say – swept straight into your being like a favourite symphony as soon as you walked into it.

But it was walking down the side of the nave and coming across stone steps, worn down by the footsteps of an endless procession of pilgrims, and moving through ancient shadows that I felt something of the real spirit of the place. I turned and turned and felt the era after era of prayer that must have flowed up through this warren of archway, alley and cloister. I noted the cleanliness and smelled the polish and saw the sheen on the wood and understood the pure love that had been poured into every inch and corner. I could even faintly hear the canticles of the monks of old.

I suppose it was in that cathedral – perhaps more than any other – that I had a sense of how much buildings grow like multiplying amoeba over the years. Wherever I looked I could see how a bit of this had been added to a bit of that, all somehow cohering into a graceful, even holy whole.

The cathedral's most unusual feature was the striking number and variety of the chantries, chapels and tombs. Painted effigies of bishops lay in perfect Plantagenet repose. Knights stretched out with their legs crossed. A shrieking, skeletal figure on one tomb looked so charred and upset he might have just been pulled off the electric chair in Sing Sing. A few mortuary chests contained the bones of Anglo-Saxon kings even, some say, those of King Canute. North of the nave was the tombstone of that marvellous novelist and princess of irony, Jane Austen.

My favourite part was the lovely grey altar screen, so detailed and elaborate it might have been modelled on a great waterfall or even Niagara herself. If you gazed at it for long enough and began blinking it really did seem to run.

This cathedral was built on the cult of St Swithun and here, again, we come across a rather different sort of saint. He performed no great miracles, nor did he scourge the land with fiery prophecies; in fact, he was an unparalleled celebration of human ordinariness. He was born in Winchester in 800 and, even when he became bishop, he only ever ate plain food and travelled around on foot. He built chapels and houses for the poor and asked that, on his death, he should be buried outside the cathedral without pomp or ceremony, where the rain fell and feet trod. He died in 862 and was buried in the churchyard.

He lay there for around a hundred years until the Bishop of Winchester, clearly keen to cash in on the pilgrim cult, ordered his remains to be brought inside. On the day the body was to be removed, July 15, 971, it rained so hard – and continued to rain so hard – that the body could not be moved for 40 days.

In that rain, it was believed, were the tears of the old saint anguishing at his disturbance. Even today it is believed by some that, if it rains on St Swithun's Day, it will then rain ferociously and without stopping for 40 days.

I went down to St Swithun's shrine at the rear of the nave. Cromwell cleared it out and had the gall to later complain that the jewels were fakes. It is not absolutely certain where the old saint's feretory was placed though there was some sort of horrible contraption on the supposed spot, just sitting there sadly like a space ship built on the cheap and out of petrol.

Much of the area is now cold and unadorned, rather different from the way it must have been once when the pilgrim would have approached a whole riot of mural colours and masses of gaudy ornaments. Yet the remains of some of the original wall paintings can still be seen in the Chapel of the Holy Sepulchre and the Guardian Angels' Chapel. Here, from the ceiling, dozens of big-eyed angels gaze down at you.

The carvings on the stall-ends of one of the chapels show what the pilgrims were like: fat, thin and disagreeable; on foot and horseback; rich and poor; aristocratic and working class. All as different and individual as a fingerprint.

Stop and listen. Hush and you can hear their footsteps even now as the pilgrims come, with a gambler's hope in their hearts, that they will be cured of ills and their souls saved by the sacred bones of St Swithun. See them now stretching their hands through a Holy Hole to touch those precious bones before getting on the road again and making the long and arduous journey to Canterbury.

But before setting out for Canterbury any modern pilgrim must first visit the Hospital of St Cross and Almshouse of Noble Poverty, just down the road in St Cross. Apart from being one of the oldest institutions in the land, it was probably the first staging post for the journey to Canterbury where, even today, the pilgrims can still claim the Wayfarers' Dole; a meal of bread and beer.

It is a curious complex of buildings, erected in 1136 by Bishop Henry Blois as a soup kitchen after the failure of the harvest. It has a huge chapel and an old quadrant of flats topped by high, almost industrial chimneys where 25 brothers – eight red coats of the Noble Poverty Foundation and 17 black coats of the Hospital Foundation – are now living together in reasonably amicable retirement.

This was the place that inspired Hiram's Hospital in Anthony Trollope's great work on the twin perils of Christianity and senility, *The Warden*. It features in his other Barchester novels as well and, on looking around trying to find someone, I half expected Obadiah Slope to come sliming around the corner at any second. Instead, I found the caretaker who gloried in the wonderfully Trollopian name of Mr Heavens.

'We still give out the bread and beer to pilgrims, oh yes,' he said to my enquiry.

I stood waiting and arranged a sort of hungry gleam on my face.

'Go on, you've got to ask.'

'Ask for what? What do I say?'

'You just ask for the dole. All you've got to do is ask for the dole.'

'Can I have the dole?'

'Oh most certainly you can. It would be my pleasure. Yes.'

Mr Heavens tottered off into his office and came back holding a round wooden salver with a small cube of bread on it and a tiny glass containing such a small drop of beer it wouldn't have got a fairy drunk. 'It's just symbolic now,' he said when I expressed a few misgivings about the size of the meal. 'Just a token, you know.'

And so, fortified by a tiny cube of bread and a tot of flat beer, I set out to follow the Pilgrim's Way, taking the North Gate out of Winchester and following the Jewry Road, so-called because it was formerly the centre of the Jewish community in the city – or so it said in the book which I was using to follow the Way, *The Old Road* by Hilaire Belloc. I went past a statue of King Alfred hoisting his sword aloft, ambled past a closed pub, made a deft swerve around some dog mess and I was on my way.

Winter had caught the land in a relentless clamp and the lanes were as quiet and dull as council planners. Now and then chilly winds erupted through the bare hedgerows, hissing venomously and firing out tons of dead brown leaves which shot around me like so many fusillades of bullets. Everywhere the earth was thick with chalk, slippery and difficult to walk on, even in my studded walking boots. The branches of the trees hung over me like cat o'nine tails.

I passed a wood with a sign saying: BEWARE OF ADDERS, though I would have thought any self-respecting adder would have been curled up and fast asleep in its warm hole at this time of year. Practically nothing was growing anywhere – just the pendulous catkins shaking in the breeze and the odd, snowy waterfall of old man's beard on some of the trees. In one churchyard, however, I did find a shy stammering of snowdrops.

It was the sheer emptiness of this chalk-dotted landscape that was so forbidding. No one was out in the fields and slivers of ice glittered in pools in ditches. Soft winds moaned quietly in the dead brown bracken. Rooks sat around in one tree, now and then exploding into knowing parliamentarian guffaws. The bang of a shotgun rang across the fields, its echo moving emptily along the side of the wood, making the rooks rise up in a black circling cloud before they settled back down again.

The joints of my none-too-fit legs were squeaking a bit when I finally signed into the Swan Hotel in New Alresford, the same town where Belloc spent his first night on the same journey. This was a very English sort of place with foot scrapers outside the doorways and curtains so thick you couldn't see inside the houses. One of the pubs had lots of ferocious animal traps dangling off the wall together with a group of farmers hogging the fire, slapping their thighs with big red hands and chortling a lot at loud blue jokes.

Down in Old Alresford I found a lovely old church, St Mary the Virgin, where I discovered, on a memorial plaque, one

Mary Summer had, in 1876, formed the Mothers' Union here. It was the first of many pleasant discoveries in what was to turn into a massive church-crawl. I came to love those moments when, after getting the keys from the rectory if the church was locked, I could wander around those old damp places alone. Usually I was tense with the expectancy of being disturbed, but I always read the Bible left open on the lectern to see what had hit the congregation the Sunday before. Sometimes I found notes on the sermon or sweet papers secreted behind a pew.

Those old English churches were jam-packed with surprises: a scratch dial near the door, for instance, by which the sun would show the times of various ancient services. I found a church on that journey which had been run by a vicar who had invented the multiplication sign and another where there was a plaque in the porch commemorating the theft of a statue by 'persons unknown'. Always, but always, you found a beautiful spray of freshly cut flowers somewhere near the altar.

Sir Arthur Bryant, in another English country church, wrote: 'All English history – its strength, its sleeping fires, its patient consistency – is here, contained in its speaking silence.'

The next morning was warm and welcoming with the dull coin of the sun making a valiant attempt to break through the thin clouds. I made my way out past watercress fields, geometric terraces with damp green clumps of cress and flowing rivulets of water laughing from one level to the next. At one time they produced so much of the stuff here the local railway line, which took it to London, was known as The Watercress Line.

I wandered on towards Alton. A dog came bursting out a garden yapping its head off. I withdrew back down the lane, which was clearly a mistake, since the beast, emboldened by my cowardice, came after me. I changed tack and began barking and growling, running straight at him and waving my bag around. He took off faster than a four-bob rocket.

Sunshine was bejewelling the dew still thick on the fields and I was no longer certain I was on the Old Road. Every time

I thought I was heading in the right direction the track disappeared into a ploughed field or ran into a brick wall or deep, snouzling river. Sometimes you could follow it through a wood and then it came to a dual carriageway with traffic zipping back and forth. All I knew for certain was I was stumbling eastwards to Canterbury.

Later that afternoon I signed into Alton Abbey for the night, finding my feet had begun to bleed not to mention several rioting patches of blisters. My left knee was giving me murder too.

Yet it immediately became clear that, although also Benedictine, this place was not another Quarr since the monks here spoke to you and smiled a lot. Indeed Brother Francis, a cherubic man with a cherubic smile, would not shut up. He was a man on whom the vow of silence would hang as easily as a death sentence, you fancied. He told me all about the place and how they had a television and were even now hoping to get a video. A *what*? They also, I learned with mounting horror, were much taken by the idea of having a microwave oven. What kind of monastery do you call this then?

They didn't bother to try and grow their own vegetables any more – 'It's just too expensive' – and neither had they any animals. 'We used to have three peacocks here,' Brother Francis explained. 'But they used to make a shocking noise until one night they were unwise enough to get on the window of the Abbot's bedroom and wake him up. They went soon after that.' They also had beehives but they were empty too.

There were four other guests in the Guest House – all college friends and ministers who met for a week each year to revive and encourage one another. It turned out that one of them kept bees. 'They only sting if you get in their flight path.' He'd had a queen bee die on him recently so he'd had a new one sent to him for five pounds. It came through the post buzzing inside a match box. The problem then was to get the bees to accept their new queen. Sometimes they did and sometimes they just flung her out through the door. That's what they did to the one who came in the match box. The rotten lot just killed her and flung her out of the front door. And one perfectly good fiver down the drain.

Royalists will doubtless be pleased to learn that complete social anarchy followed this dastardly act with the whole structure of the hive going to the dogs, workers doing no work, soldiers messing about when they should have been on guard duty and nothing much by the way of honey being produced.

The Alton monks did, however, run an old people's home as well as generating further income from making communion wafers and incense. This operation was run by Brothers Benedict and Bede – a sort of holy Morecambe and Wise. Brother Benedict explained that, together, the two of them turned out some hundred thousand wafers a month, making up the paste, baking it into sheets and punching holes in them with their shining new machine. 'We just had that old puncher before.'

When the Pope came they worked their little sandals off, making half a million wafers for the Coventry Mass alone. The Carmelites make most of the wafers with Alton filling in the gaps. 'No, we couldn't start assembling colour televisions or anything like that. Our work has to be compatible with religious life.'

Brother Benedict also took me to his little cobwebbed room, a sort of scented Prospero's cell where he made up his special incense mixtures such as Rosa Mystica, Madonna, Festival and Special, all at £6.90 per pound plus V.A.T. He let me sniff some of his ingredients such as essence of geranium, hyacinth, sandalwood, jasmine and lavender. I took a good sniff on his patchouli and said it reminded me of a Bombay brothel. Realizing I was speaking to a holy man I flushed but he merely took the vial off me, sniffed it and said, 'Yes, I suppose it does.'

So what did a Benedictine monk in Alton Abbey know about a Bombay brothel?

Oh, I would be surprised at what he knew, he said, since he had once sailed in the Merchant Navy with Shaw Saville and Union Castle lines. I too had once worked for both those lines as a seaman, as it happened, and our eyes briefly caught each

other's; an odd moment to be sure – two men discussing incense
in a monastery and, in a spasm of common insight, realizing we
both knew of a world which was as far removed from holiness
and incense as it was possible to get.

After the evening service, I chatted with the Abbot, Mark
Gibson, a large man seemingly built out of circles with bullfrog
jowls and a surprising light music in his voice. It was while talking to him that I understood why the abbey was so happy and
relaxed: the boss was happy as the day was long with a permanent smile on his lips which seemed to have rubbed off on
everyone.

'I find television a good way to relax,' he smiled when I
asked him why he was allowing his charges to watch the box so
much. 'I recently had an accident and spent all day watching
television. It was lovely. Now they're all saying they want a
video so I suppose I'll let them have one.'

I thought such things were terrible in a monastery and
bound to turn them into an Athenian rabble.

'Well, you're quite wrong on that, since Benedictine monas-
teries have always been in the vanguard of the modern world.
Benedict always saw us as adapting to the world we live in. It
was not part of God's plan that we live in sixth-century Italy.'

They'd be reading newspapers next, I sneered.

'Oh yes, we do that too. Brother Francis likes to read newspapers. They give him subjects for intercessory prayers.'

The trouble with these monks is they've all been given
Jesuitical training and they've got an answer for everything.

The morning sun was breaking through cloud and whispering
enthralling promises of a coming spring when I left the abbey.
At the bottom of the hill I passed a white Siamese cat with
huge blue eyes sitting in a patch of sunlight by a privet hedge.
Then I came to the town of Alton itself, a charming mish-mash
of the old and new, sitting at the head of the Wey Valley with
a fine chapel and a church door, still battle-scarred after coming

under fire by the Roundheads. The grammar school came and
went and I was soon back on my wintry chalk landscape again.

Today, I was on the Pilgrim's Way for sure. It followed the
main road from Alton to Farnham, right next to the same river
that provided water for the pilgrims of old to drink and wash
in. Hilaire Belloc claimed there were three main factors in the
survival of the Old Way: the pilgrims themselves, the eighteenth-
century turnpike system – which meant that travellers would
want to avoid toll charges on the main roads – and, most
importantly, the chalk. This viscous, spongy stuff, he said,
would have been shaped by the endless procession of walking
feet. The chalk would always hold the shape of the Old Road;
indeed, you could often spot the trail scything through the
hillside ahead of you.

Belloc wrote:

> The chalk is our landscape and our proper habitation. The
> chalk filtered our drink for us and built up our strong bones;
> it was the height from the slopes of which our villages, stand-
> ing in a clear air, could watch the sea or plain; we carved
> it – when it was hard enough; it holds our first ornaments;
> our clear streams run over it; the shapes and curves it takes
> and the kind of close rough grass it bears (an especial grass
> for sheep), are the cloak of our counties; its lonely breadths
> delight us when the white flocks and clouds move over them
> together; where the waves break into the cliffs, they are the
> characteristic of our shores, and through its thin coat of
> whitish mould go thirsty roots of our three trees – the
> beech, the holly and the yew.

The last few miles into Farnham were hell. My left knee had all
but packed up and I could barely walk as I hobbled into the
first hotel I came across, The Bishop's Table. It was hideously
expensive but, when I complained, the manager knocked five
pounds off the nightly rate. Grateful for small mercies I put
myself to bed for a couple of days to let my knee heal.

It was a grey, sobbing morning when I picked up the Old Way again in the village of Seale, nestling in a vale in the shadow of the Hog's Back. It was a place of some charm populated, I guessed, by retired brigadiers and those who had finally hung up their bowler hats. The church had a 600-year-old porch and, in one corner, a copy of the will of one John Fylpot who, in January 1487, bequeathed his soul to God, tuppence to the cathedral in Winchester, a further tuppence to the high altar, one sheep to the light of the cross, one sheep to the light of St Nicholas and one sheep to the light of St Lawrence.

Later I had a chat with the verger but barely recalled a word he said since that morning I had received some news which had broken my heart. My great hero and spiritual mentor, Canon David Watson, had died.

All deaths claw at our insides and some more than others but the loss of David was particularly shattering for me. Not only had he helped to lead me back to Christ, he had also lit the path for hundreds, if not thousands, of others. He was one of the great pilgrims of history and I counted meeting him one of the real privileges of my life. The man seethed with honesty and integrity. I had long believed and prayed that he would be healed of his cancer so he could lead our lost and fallen tribe back to God. But now he was dead. Why?

I trudged sadly onward when I came across a lovely old Saxon church in Compton and sat alone in a wooden pew, looking up at the stout round pillars fashioned out of chalk, the chancel arch and the strange, possibly unique double sanctuary. There was one beautiful piece of stained glass – one of the earliest in the country, it said in the guidebook. 'The green robe of the saviour was similar to the ancient glass at York Minster.'

York. Ah yes. It was in York that I had first met David. It was in York that his work had become a symbol for renewal in the Anglican Church. His church was far from dead and you had to come early to get a seat. Such beautiful moments in the worship, as I remembered – the swelling joy of the singing, the eddying flute in the Communion and David's jokes. Funny jokes too, told by a man with big jug ears, an enormous nose, a rich, full voice and eyes that disappeared into slits when he laughed.

Many times that year I felt I had come close to the practice and presence of God but sitting in that old Saxon church in Compton I felt I knew nothing at all about him. I understood only the darkness of the dark night. God told us that his thoughts are not our thoughts but, at times that year, I had felt close to his healing power though now he had clearly withdrawn again, leaving me shivering and chattering helplessly in the cold and damp. He had withdrawn and, outside, a grey winter rain was falling on everything.

The real problem – the main, jagged irony – was that I did not now think I could turn my back on God either. I was not at all sure even in my bitterness and anger at him – that I could find the time and energy to stamp him out of my heart again. But I did, that day, understand his aloofness and that old monk at Quarr who had said: 'He's nothing like his created reality. The closer you come, the further away he seems to be. The more you know the more you realize that you don't understand at all. He is only like himself.'

A lonely, stumbling walk into Guildford. Dark trees stared down at the howling in my knee and the savage crumbling in my heart. The empty dusk had no pity. The streetlamps and lights of passing cars sent my shadow dancing all around. Shadows ambled towards me when I approached the streetlamps. Shadows raced around me when the cars passed by. My breath plumed around me in white vapours. I simply wanted to lie down right there on the pavement and die.

The next morning I woke up in Guildford to find that my get-up-and-go had well and truly got up and gone. I had clearly got some cartilage trouble in my knee and the means of finishing this journey was by hiring a car. A car! What a rotten leg of my pilgrimage this was turning out to be. But there seemed to be no other option; I could hardly crawl those remaining miles.

So I hired a car and my first day back behind the wheel was

hardly worth bothering about. I was now unable to finish the Old Way continuously and had to drive up here and double back around there, picking up what I could. To make matters worse I often took the wrong turning and ended up on the motorway which ran almost next to the Old Way, sometimes having to make a ten-mile detour to get back where I wanted to be.

What could be more depressingly different from the journey of the pilgrims of old than driving down a motorway? One day I was wandering along catkin lanes, struggling through clouds of pilgrim prayer and memory and now I was whizzing about in a little tin box, trussed up with a seat belt like a battery hen, with not a soul to pass the time of day with.

Where once I could sit and rest on a bank of dead fern I now sat looking at mile after mile of unwinding concrete, belting its way through the countryside at odds with everything. There was none of the society of those old coaching inns in the motorway cafés either – just people coming in for a quick bite, many so mesmerized by the constant movement of their windscreen wipers they acted and moved like zombies, others queuing up for food with globby piles of chips stacked on everything and coffee machines where you had to press half a dozen buttons before getting half a cup of cold tea.

When I finally picked up the old pilgrim track again I came to St Martha's Hill, leaving the car and hobbling up through a wood, past an abandoned chalk pit, unsung and silent and given over to ivy, to find the church locked and the view of the surrounding countryside, said to be the finest in the county, obscured by rain mists.

Later in the day, mooching around another churchyard, I spotted scoops of earth flying up out of the ground and I went over for a chat with the gravedigger, a young art student with fine features and an even finer attitude. 'I've got to go down really deep for this one,' he told me. 'The husband's going down tomorrow and I've got leave enough room for the wife. It's tough stuff this clay but not as wet as it is on the other side. Sometimes I have little turns when I come across some old bones but I just put them in a polythene bag and let the vicar deal with them. No, I don't know what he does with them. Myself, I want to be cremated. I've seen too much of the dirty side of this business to want to be put down here. And it's expensive. You've got pay a basic £400 for the cheapest funeral and then you can go up to £1,000 with no problem. I wouldn't want my family to spend all that just to get rid of my dead bones.'

I drove onwards, still rumbling with my own grief, past yet more damp churches and pools where pilgrims would have stopped to drink. One man who lived near some lime workings said that around a hundred pilgrims a day came walking past his house in the summer. 'They're often knocking on the door and asking for a drink of water. Lots of them do it on that so-much-a-mile sponsorship deal. I don't mind them asking for water. It's when they leave crisp packets and litter everywhere that I object.'

Later that afternoon I signed into a Carmelite monastery, The Friars in Aylesford, a tangle of old buildings and stately archways, set around a bird-songed courtyard and next to a peaceful sweep of the River Medway. Geese wandered unconcernedly on the main path leading up to the monastery. Doves warbled in the eaves and, out in the front of the reception office, the leaves of a solitary acacia tree chattered in the cold wind.

Of all religious orders the Carmelites are perhaps most closely associated with the pilgrim cult. They first gathered as a disorganized band of pilgrims on the slopes of Mount Carmel in Israel where, in the tradition of Old Testament prophets, they maintained a life of prayer and silence. A small party of them later came to settle in Aylesford in 1242.

My guide around the place, another Brother Francis, was a man with a shy, quiet personality which sat strangely in his huge all-in wrestler's body. First he took me to the tremendous Pilgrims' Hall, probably the oldest building in the priory and now used for meals. It has two wooden upper galleries with neo-Elizabethan rafters and it would have been on these galleries that three to four hundred pilgrims a night would have slept on their way to Canterbury. Youth groups still sleep here when they make a similar journey.

Brother Francis also showed me the Prior's Hall with its series of paintings by the Polish artist, Adam Kossowski, outlining the history of the Carmelites. The adjoining cloister chapel was now used for silent prayer and meditation and the stained glass window was a gift from the artist Moira Forsyth. We moved on over to the new shrine with the choir chapel now being used daily for the Mass and Office of the church. Nearly a quarter of a million pilgrims come here each year to worship in the open-air church. Large groups have also come from Poland, Italy and Spain, though the Spaniards are not going to be allowed back. 'They left too much rubbish behind them last time,' Brother Francis whispered.

The main shrine, to which most flocked, was the Relic Chapel. On the altar stood a reliquary containing St Simon's skull and it was visible even now, sitting behind some thick plate glass, looking like a rough, reddish coconut as it perched on a tiny white pillow put there, one suspects, to make it feel comfortable. 'It's not much fun being a saint,' said Brother Francis. 'Bits of you get scattered everywhere. As you can see, we got the skull.'

After supper I had a long chat with the Prior, Edward Maguire, a man with a puckish red face and silvery curling hair and such an attitude of having lived life to the hilt he might have been a Montmartre painter or a Greenwich Village drunk. He had been here for nine years and it soon emerged that he was a man with a lively and shrewd intelligence.

What they did here, he explained, was take people in who needed help. 'Exhausted people, alcoholics. We give them a warm room and feed them and give them time to reflect on their lives. We don't take in people who have just had a nervous breakdown since the quiet and isolation wouldn't help. There's always some sort of transient population here. We never send anyone away. This is simply a place of prayer.'

The conversation drifted to the death of David Watson. I said I was exhausted too. And very angry with God.

'Well, anger with God is fine. That's a form of prayer too. And if you are angry with him you should always tell him so. It's even a form of passionate prayer. But remember he is not as we are. We each of us have sparks that we hand on to one another. That's all I know for certain. Your weaknesses are always detected and become someone else's strength. In some strange way we are always looking after one another. Somehow there is a sense in which suffering always fulfils God's purpose. But how? I couldn't even start to tell you why six million Jews were allowed to die in Germany. Your mind will not be able to help you with the loss of this man. You won't be able to think your way out of it. Neither is it so much a matter of time as a matter of acceptance when you will find a pattern, a reason. Then you will be able to take it.'

They were the good, concerned words of a good, concerned man. That night in my bed they rang in my mind, a poultice, at least, on the still suppurating boil of my grief.

People often ask me if I write about places in advance of actually seeing them. The answer is no, never. A writer who succumbs to his prepackaged notions will soon get into a load of trouble not to mention a further load of hard work changing them back again.

But that year I had often fantasized about my final few miles into Canterbury and it went something like this:

It would have been a long dog of a tramp all day as I moved down the Old Way with just the sheep looking at me. When my tired body and bleeding feet announced they could go no further, I would round a bend and my spirits would soar as I first spotted the spire of Canterbury Cathedral rising, majestic and mysterious, out of flower-flecked fields. The land would be covered by low-lying mists too. Earlier that day there had been a shower of rain which, even now, the sun was drying out.

I would have to decide if I was to stop for the night there so that I could tackle this spiritual queen of the cities fresh, first thing in the morning, or if I should press on. Still unsure I would have knocked up a friendly vicar in a huge stone local rectory, full of damp and mildewed theological books, where he would have stuffed me with marvellous food and fabulous stories, whereupon, suitably revived, I would have tramped off into the thickening dusk and straight up to the cathedral door where, with bats flitting around me, I would have slumped to my knees and given thanks for a safe journey throughout the year.

The reality was altogether different.

I did stop at Chilham, a small snooty English town six miles out of Canterbury and the last staging post on the Old Way, only to find the church locked. I finally located the rectory – a modern, detached red-brick job with an integral garage and a dog barking inside it – but no one was in. The nearby pub was closed too so, finally, I jumped into my car and drove to Canterbury and, rather than seeing that dreaming tower poking up out of steaming rose fields, I did not see it at all since, on the city outskirts, I got stuck in a traffic jam for more than an hour because they were digging up the road.

Even worse my hire car had begun to show a distinct and worrying tendency to fall to bits. The clutch was travelling some six inches before it engaged. The radio merely screamed with static and now the lock had fallen out of the driver's door and was hanging off like a detached eyeball hanging on the end of a bit of string. It confirmed all I had ever believed about these four-wheeled boxes which had conspired to imprison and ruin the world.

On the same journey, on two feet as God had planned it, Belloc had written of his first sight of the vast cathedral with its immense spire: 'It was the pivot of all we saw. Save perhaps once at Beauvais I had never known such a magic of great height and darkness.'

No such raptures for me. When we finally got over a bridge, past a clanking steamroller and a man waving a green flag, through that appalling smell of boiling tar and past men with shovels flinging asphalt around, we were detoured off the main road and through an industrial estate. When I did spot the cathedral's great spire, it was poking up over the dowdy orange asbestos roof of a factory making kitchen fittings. Chaucer and his gang couldn't have had this kind of trouble.

It was dusk when I signed into the Falstaff Hotel near the West Gate, an appropriate enough choice of watering hole, since the gate was always locked at nightfall in Chaucer's time. Visiting pilgrims had to wait out here in one of the inns or alehouses until dawn. But the gate is no longer locked for the night curfew, of course, so I ventured out into the dark city streets for a night of quiet celebration now I had finished my year-long journey.

I found Canterbury an attractive and cheerful jumble of brick and half-timbered houses with moneyed, rather self-conscious fashion shops, a sprinkling of pubs without much life in the bars and sudden, surprising aspects of waterways flowing behind the backs of wonky houses built in the Middle Ages.

The next morning I ventured back into the city hoping to locate the Chequers of Hope with its dormitory of a hundred beds. This was where Chaucer and his fellow pilgrims had stayed: that colourful, motley crowd which included a prioress, a nun, three priests, the monk and the friar. Then there was the scholar, a pardoner, a summoner, a cook, a haberdasher, carpenter, weaver and tapestry-maker not forgetting the miller, the parson, the reeve, the frankelyn and 'a verray parfit gentil knyght'.

No such persons were out on the wintry streets that morning though there were some schoolboys with starched, butterfly collars, a sprinkling of American tourists and tradesmen carting their goods to a weekly trade fair. 'This is the worst trade fair of them all,' one trader told another. 'They think it's just Woolworth's. When did you ever make money in Canterbury?'

The Chequers of Hope no longer exists though there are a

few of its paving stones in a coffee shop beneath a new department store. I did, however, find one genuine curiosity – a huge, red pump, pinned to a wall above the window of a leather shop. This pump, I had been told, commemorated the monks' practice of selling medieval pilgrims water red with rust. The monks claimed the water was tainted with the blood of Thomas à Becket.

The man in the Tourist Information Shop, Gavin MacLean, did not know if this story was true but he did explain that increasing numbers of pilgrims – largely from America, France and Holland – were now coming here each year. Some thirty-two thousand came to his shop last year alone. Having ascertained the size of their wallets he would direct them to accommodation that ranged from Mrs Wainwright in South Canterbury Road who charged £5 a night, to the four-star County Hotel where two nights' bed and breakfast would cost more than most people earn in a week.

Clearly times had changed since 1520, when a poster was set up in the street to display the provisions made with 'letters expressing the ordering of vitell and lodging for pylgrymes'. Then they might have slept three to a bed with three beds to a room. Some would have slept on straw-filled palliasses and had to cope with fleas and mice.

A siren wind blew in freezing gusts around the flat lawns of the cathedral when I finally entered the precincts. I looked up at the great Norman arcadings and ornate stone traceries. Inside, I was immediately overwhelmed by the sheer size of the nave. There was little intimacy here but – as befits the Mother Church of Anglican Christendom – there was unmistakable authority.

Machines offering earphone commentaries for twenty pence were dotted around in white metal banks. Two students were sharing one earpiece. Tourists drifted past, one with a crying baby. One hiker had coloured badges stitched to his rucksack

– Monte Carlo, Morocco, Paris, Spain. One supposed that such men, with their mountainous backpacks and legs like oak trees, were the real modern pilgrims. Pilgrims of old would have gone to Jerusalem, Rome and Santiago de Compostela.

Footsteps and voices echoed around the stone columns of the crypt. A child dropped a sweet paper and was told to pick it up. Two black-gowned vergers were discussing a forthcoming concert. A woman was praying alone in one of the small chapels and there was an enormous range of merchandise for sale in the shop.

The stained glass was astonishing, perhaps the finest I had seen anywhere all year. It was so careful in its detail, so brilliant in its texture, so certain in its faith it made me catch my breath. Hands stood out like beacons. Faces shone like the sun. Here those four mad knights slaughtered Thomas à Becket, whose shrine at the far end of the cathedral stood as empty and silent as the looted tomb it was. They needed 26 carts to carry all the treasures away when it was Dissolved.

Christendom reacted with tremendous emotion to this savage murder and Thomas was made a saint within days of his death. Miraculous cures were soon reported near the tomb, children were christened Thomas, stained glass windows proclaimed his glory as thousands upon thousands made their way here to be baptized in the font of their own tears.

In the high noon of medieval pilgrimage this shrine was covered with gold plate and jewels of every kind – rubies, emeralds, sapphires and diamonds. All these surrounded the 'brain pan of the holy martyr'. The relic trade also underwent a boom with parts of Thomas' clothing going far and wide – his books and penknife to Bury, a tooth to Verona. A Florence convent claimed to have an arm, blithely ignoring Lisbon's claim they already had them both. The racket in indulgences prospered too.

Henry VIII, the Defender of the Faith, dissolved the shrine and so the Canterbury pilgrims' wonderland came to an end after four and a half centuries. But Dissolution was just as well.

It marked the end of a corrupt and decadent church which had become an offence to God. There was an historic inevitability, I came to learn on my pilgrimage, in the arrival of men like Calvin, Knox and Luther. They were ecclesiastical doctors sent to purge the poisoned body.

But who now was going to purge the present church which is not so much corrupt as fast asleep; not so much decadent as divided? Such a church is just as much an enemy of God as a decadent one, as ineffective as that cordoned-off empty space now before me. In many ways this looted tomb was a perfect symbol of that which ministers to us now – a forlorn emptiness echoing to the chatter of tourists and the flash of cameras.

Later I went into the Chapel of Saints and Martyrs and lit a candle for that great canon, saint and martyr, David Watson. The flame shone a bright yellow with hazy stammering smoke drifting up out of its tip before settling again. Light flickered on the brown marble pillar behind. He had all the qualities of the saints of old did David. Just like Swithun, who travelled around on foot, David only ever travelled around on a bicycle and ate the simplest of meals. Like Patrick, David also fought the demons of darkness with prayer and fasting. Like Columba – 'tender in every adversity' – he was always prepared to teach even when 'hurting, wounded and vulnerable'. Like Cuthbert, he taught goodness by the impeccable lesson of being good himself. His spirit straddled the modern world – albeit tragically briefly – just as surely as the spirits of those medieval saints.

Holiness abides. That's all I really learned about holiness on my journey beneath wild Saxon skies and along Celtic paths. Institutions may fall and decay and the loved old may give way to the despised new but there will always be men ready to pick up the fallen torch, always another to pass it on and teach us again the way and meaning of holiness.

When I left the cathedral groups of visitors were hanging back in the porch. It was snowing. Huge fat flakes came whirling in over the grey rooftops, falling softly on my face and dissolving in my eyes like tears. Two schoolboys rattled past on